T0279696

Adoption is a complicated issue. Penny subject of an adoption and search history book to set the record straight. And *Greek, Actually* accomplishes that goal masterfully: Penny refuses to be a victim but takes back agency of her story and history, and of all the upheavals and emotions in between. Penny also adds ample research material and policy documentation, which take the reader well beyond her personal case, to leave an informed warning against the type of cross-border adoption that should never be repeated. This book is an homage to human resilience and to the importance of identity rights.

—Gonda Van Steen, author of *Adoption, Memory, and Cold War Greece* and Koraes Professor, King's College London

A compelling narrative of an adoptee's relentless perseverance in her search for identity and belonging in the face of repeated rejections. Penny raises numerous issues including the ultimate question of the future of adoption.

—The Honourable Nahum Mushin AM, Former Chair, Commonwealth Government's Forced Adoptions Apology Reference Group

This is much more than a story. It is a record, a textbook, a guide, a testament, a learning. It is essential practical reading to not only understand the complexity of adoption but the shortcomings of contemporary views of related practices. This book is a triumph.

—Ted Baillieu, Former Premier of Victoria

Dr Zagarelou-Mackieson has written an important and gripping tale of her journey out of the adoption labyrinth and her heroic determination and compassion shines through at every turn. A must-read for every person who has ever wondered what all the fuss about being adopted is and who loves a good Australian yarn, albeit one that is stranger than fiction; an incredible true story written with courage, compassion, humour and flair. *Greek, Actually* also comes with a wealth of information that will be an invaluable resource for students looking to understand Australia's complex and cruel adoption history.

—Dr Catherine Lynch JD, Adoptee Rights Australia, Inc.

In writing her story, Zagarelou-Mackieson walks us through the long and complicated journey to find her biological family. The complexity of this adoption story compels the reader to walk in the shoes of those who have to navigate the many injustices that adoptees must manage in order to find that one person, their birth mother.

—Jennifer Lahl, President, The Center for Bioethics and Culture

From Penny Zagarelou-Mackieson comes an honest, sobering, and straightforward testament to what it feels like to be an adopted person and what it means to fight for transparency, accuracy and accountability in the right to know who you are and from whom you come. In *Greek, Actually*, Zagarelou-Mackieson chronicles the careless, painful missteps in her own adoption journey, which leads to the realization that the birth mother and family she found and had come to know, were not hers at all. Difficult and heartbreaking, but also triumphant, this book puts another spotlight on the argument for open access to birth records for adoptees. As Zagarelou-Mackieson learns her true identity over time, she reminds us, once again, of this human rights issue, which affects millions of children around the world who are displaced through the practice of adoption. This is an important read. Adopted people have pasts. Without the reconciliation of those pasts, adoptees can never be whole, can never be at peace. Thank you, Penny Zagarelou-Mackieson.

—Dr Mary Cardaras is a Greek-born adoptee and adoptee activist and is the author of *Ripped at the Root* and editor of *Voices of the Lost Children of Greece*

The book is a detailed account of the struggle of Penny to find her original identity, connect with her roots and then integrate it all in her life and being. It is an important book as it raises awareness about the effects of changing the identity of children and the long journey for adoptees to reclaim their identity.

—Arun Dohle, Executive Director, Against Child Trafficking
www.againstchildtrafficking.org

Dr Penny Zagarelou-Mackieson is an Australian author who lives with her husband and their son in inner Melbourne. Penny attained social work qualifications from the University of Melbourne and worked for three decades primarily in the child and family services sector. Penny's PhD research explored Permanent Care Orders for children in Victoria's child protection and out-of-home care system. Penny was adopted in Victoria as a newborn in 1963 and 'de-adopted' in 2022. Penny served from 2014 to 2019 on the board of VANISH Inc., a community-based organisation providing search and support services to family members separated through adoption.

Other books by Penny Zagarelou-Mackieson

Real Women Love Footy
(co-authored with Dawn Leicester)
2003

Adoption Deception:
A Personal and Professional Journey
2015

GREEK,
ACTUALLY

Disentangling Adoption Deceptions

Penny Zagarelou-Mackieson

We respectfully acknowledge the wisdom of Aboriginal and
Torres Strait Islander peoples and their custodianship of the lands
and waterways. The Countries on which Spinifex offices are
situated are Djiru, Bunurong and Wurundjeri, Wadawurrung,
Gundungarra and Noongar.

First published by Spinifex Press, 2023
Spinifex Press Pty Ltd
PO Box 200, Little River, VIC 3211, Australia
PO Box 105, Mission Beach, QLD 4852, Australia
women@spinifexpress.com.au
www.spinifexpress.com.au

Edited by Susan Hawthorne, Pauline Hopkins and Renate Klein
Cover design by Deb Snibson
Typesetting by Helen Christie, Blue Wren Books
Typeset in Minion Pro
Printed in the USA

A catalogue record for this
book is available from the
National Library of Australia

ISBN: 9781925950793 (paperback)
ISBN: 9781925950809 (ebook)

For all my families.

"It's sweet to view the sea when standing on the shore."
Archippus, Early Greek Christian

ACKNOWLEDGEMENTS

I owe many thanks in relation to this book.

I am grateful to the team at the Victorian Government's Adoption Information Service for all they have done in helping me traverse the complexities of my unexpected discovery in relation to my origins. I am especially grateful to Angela Karavidas for her instrumental role in engaging members of my maternal family in Greece. Without Ange, this story would have ended far too soon, with far too many questions and far too few answers.

I am grateful to Martin Flanagan for his wise counsel in helping me work out when I was ready to start writing this story.

I am grateful to all the team at Spinifex Press for their commitment and expertise in publishing this book.

I am grateful to the VANISH Inc. community for their ongoing support in relation to my adoption saga, especially Pauline Ley, Charlotte Smith and Simon Pryor.

I am deeply grateful to my partner, Bruce Minahan, and our son, Patrick Minahan, for always being there for me, for their unconditional embrace of my (and Patrick's) Greek heritage, and for enthusiastically sharing our first experience of Greece together. Ευχαριστώ κύριοι!

I am also grateful to my good friends, Veronica Sakell and her Bruce (Gemmell), Jenny McAuley and Catherine Neville, for also being there for me on so many levels, and for sharing my early experiences of Greece with me. Ευχαριστω φιλοι μου!

CONTENTS

INTRODUCTION

This book is autobiographical. To be clear, the book refers to other parties impacted by what happened to me and how I responded. However, it does not endeavour to narrate their experiences—each party impacted will have their own perspective on the facts related here.

As described in *Adoption Deception* (2015), my experience in personal and professional spheres converges, and significantly overlaps, in regard to adoption. *Greek, Actually* does not seek to reproduce *Adoption Deception*, but necessarily refers to its content. I emphasise that neither book was intended as a scholarly work, though both include scholarly elements. Relevant legislation, government reports, publicly available data, and a range of other academic and non-academic works are referenced to demonstrate my understanding of the subject and contextualise my experience. I hope this will help illuminate real life unintended consequences of past adoptions and current barriers to addressing them. Like other authors of this genre, I also hope that sharing my experiences will help other people deal with similar circumstances.[1]

Adoption Deception proved to be more than an accurate title for my previous book—it was prescient. Hence, my primary motivation for writing *Greek, Actually* is to set the record straight

---

1   For example, see Mike Chalek and Jessica Gardner's book, *Fraud on the Court: One Adoptee's Fight to Reclaim His Identity* (2012).

1

in the wake of the major discovery concerning my ancestry and subsequent developments since *Adoption Deception* was published in 2015. Even though I had then recently commenced PhD studies on permanent care, a topic directly relevant to adoption, I did not plan to write another book on adoption, especially not one on the topic of my own adoption. Nor did I anticipate accidentally discovering through a consumer genetic genealogy test that my mother—my natural mother, according to my official adoption records, with whom I had been 'in reunion' for almost 20 years[2]— was genetically unrelated to me.

The foundational event—my identity having been swapped with another baby's soon after birth in a Melbourne hospital prior to adoption—seems so incredible as to be fictional, such as in Channel 9's TV drama series *Love Child*.[3] The story is complicated and as events unfolded has at times felt so surreal that it could be a novel or movie plot rather than real life. Indeed, I have felt like an imposter in my own life. Many times, too, I asked how could this have happened? Why did it have to happen to me? What does it mean in the broader context? In grappling with these questions it amazes me that numerous other cases of adoptees swapped after birth during the heyday of forced and closed adoption practices in Australia have not yet come to light. Part of my rationale for this view is outlined in Chapter 1: Adoption, Deception, and DNA Questions, which was originally published under the same title as a member's contribution in the December 2020 edition of *Voice*, the regular newsletter of VANISH Inc. The version presented here

---

2   Consent was sought and received from members of the family I understood to be my natural maternal family to use their real names in *Adoption Deception*. However, the situation has changed since then and it was not appropriate to seek their consent to use their real names in *Greek, Actually*. In this book, therefore, they are referred to by alias names, rather than by their real names.
3   See 9 Entertainment's 'The 5 most heartbreaking moments from Love Child', especially Season 4, Episode 1.

in Chapter 1 includes Footnotes referencing the materials used in preparing the piece.

It is no exaggeration to say that my life has been derailed and that I've experienced a rollercoaster of emotions in relation to my ancestry discovery and the twists and turns involved in dealing with this. The impact was undoubtedly exacerbated by also having to cope with the harsh measures imposed by Australian governments in response to the COVID-19 pandemic during much of the same period. In particular, as a resident of Victoria (which "endured the most restrictive and sustained set of restrictions in Australia"[4]), and especially of Melbourne (the city that "spent the most cumulative days under stay-at-home orders" in the world[5]), during the lockdowns I felt trapped in a bubble of authoritarian deception, subjected to another outrageous violation of my human dignity under the velvet guise of paternalistic lies.

I'm now sensitive to draconian 'best interests' social policies and sceptical of decision-making processes within bureaucracies, presumably a legacy of my own personal and professional histories. As such, I did not enjoy having been made to feel as if I were uncaring and treasonous for questioning whether particular COVID-19 measures and their likely consequences were commensurate with the relevant health threat[6] and for expecting public access to the evidence and reasoning on which those measures were purportedly based. My anxiety persists in relation to the ease with which the Victorian Government—a democratically elected government—was able to introduce measures without parliamentary oversight,

---

4   Quoted from Tanya Serry, Tonya Stebbins, Andrew Martchenko, Natalie Araujo and Brigid McCarthy (10 May 2022) 'Improving Access to COVID-19 Information by Ensuring the Readability of Government Websites', p. 2.

5   Quoted from Calla Wahlquist (2 October 2021) 'How Melbourne's "Short, Sharp" Covid Lockdowns Became the Longest in the World'.

6   As Carmen Lawrence stated in her book, *Fear and Politics* (2006), p. 12: "when people are reminded of their mortality, they are more likely to exhibit increased prejudice and aggression toward those who question their beliefs, those with different worldviews, and those who are, or appear to be, different from them."

measures that blatantly breached human rights and freedoms, yet also engendered blind acceptance of anti-democratic rhetoric and policing. To me, it feels like a slippery slope toward the resumption of forced adoption policies and practices in Victoria, this time as an overt strategy intended to address the ever-growing numbers of children entering the state's struggling statutory child protection and out-of-home care systems, *à la* New South Wales (NSW).

Thankfully, the surreal feelings, the imposter feelings, and the feelings of helpless rage I've experienced in relation to my situation have now largely subsided. This was facilitated not only by the Victorian Government's political decision to abruptly drop its doomed zero-COVID-19 strategy, but also by my exercise of agency in pursuing and reclaiming my origins. Chapter 5: Chronology since 2015 provides a chronological summary of the key developments relating to my ancestry discovery juxtaposed with developments relating to the broader context of Australian and, especially, Victorian adoption policy, legislation and practice since 2015. Chapters 2 and 3 narrate the gamut of my responses to those developments. Chapter 2: Through the DNA Looking Glass focuses on the period of the gradual revelation of my genetic parentage. Chapter 3: Piecing Penny Together Again focuses on the subsequent period, which has included the search for my natural family members as well as the processes associated with integrating my identity and correcting my official records.

I attained legal recognition of my true natural identity and its integration with my adoptive identity in March 2022 despite there being no access to an integrated birth certificate for individuals adopted in Victoria. Legally I'm no longer the subject of an Adoption Order and am still figuring out how best to describe this unusual status[7]—perhaps I have become 'de-adopted'. Regardless, it

---

7   The report from the Victorian parliamentary *Inquiry Into Responses to Historical Forced Adoption in Victoria* (2021, p. 174) noted that from 2010 to 2016 there were

has been healing for me to have formally peeled back the layers of deception associated with my adoption; to have overcome the legal and bureaucratic hurdles; to have had the official lies associated with my adoptive identity undone and corrected; and to now have congruence between the true biological facts of my birth (as far as I know them) and my legal identity, and to have this accurately recorded on my birth certificate. My situation, which is still evolving, may never be all sunshine and roses but I'm grateful to have achieved sufficient peace of mind to be able to reflect on, and write about, my inadvertent discovery and subsequent responses.

As signalled by the title of this book, the major discovery concerning my ancestry is that my parentage is Greek, not Celtic-Anglo as my official adoption records led me to believe for decades. In modern times it has been argued in defence of adoption that the practice dates back to Ancient Greek (and Ancient Roman) times, but I've often wondered how much adoption proponents really know about the earliest purposes, laws and practices of adoption. The coincidence of it turning out that both adoption and I share deep Greek heritage motivated me to further explore adoption in Ancient Greece and consider similarities and differences between the intentions and legal arrangements involved there compared to now in Victoria. This exploration is presented in Chapter 4: There's a Greek Story Behind Everything. I conclude that while adoption has always been a complicated institution, not only does adoption have no clear purpose in contemporary Victoria, but arguably has no relevance either.

My human dignity has largely been restored and I feel liberated and fortified now that truth forms the scaffolding of my identity rather than official lies. However, it seems that Australians generally are comfortable with the deceptions, human rights

---

"approximately three applications to discharge an adoption per year in Victoria" and "that all applications were made by adults."

violations and stigmatising secrecy still deeply embedded in much adoption law and practice across the country. In reality, the deceptions of adoption continue to hide in plain sight and are replicated in contemporary laws and practices pertaining to third party and medically assisted reproductive technologies such as surrogacy. I would like to believe that readers unconvinced by my arguments in *Adoption Deception* to abolish adoption as we know it will reconsider their stance after reading *Greek, Actually*. But in my experience it is very difficult to convince those who subscribe to 'forever family' and 'happily-ever-after' adoption narratives that an Adoption Order is, in fact, a form of state-sanctioned identity erasure that is discriminatory, optional, unnecessary, often harmful, and not a 'right' either for intending parents or children placed in alternative care.

The Reverend Keith C. Griffith is widely quoted in the adoption community as having accurately observed that, "Adoption loss is the only trauma in the world where victims are expected by the whole of society to be grateful."[8] Mindful of the accuracy of that statement, perhaps the best I can hope for is that readers of *Greek, Actually* will be persuaded to support the human rights of adopted individuals by not opposing reforms designed to provide adults who were adopted as babies or children with easier, faster and cheaper access to de-adoption.

---

8   For example, as quoted by Mirah Riben in an article in the *Huffington Post* in 2015.

CHAPTER 1

Adoption, Deception, and DNA Questions[9]

Coercion and secrecy were common features of the up to 250,000 formal adoptions arranged in Australia from 1940 to the 1980s.[10] The population affected is substantial—it includes the adoptees, their natural and adoptive parents, siblings and extended family members, and their partners, children and subsequent descendants.

Yet, empirical research in Australia on historical forced and closed adoptions is limited,[11] and longitudinal research non-existent. Core to the small research base are several studies undertaken by the Australian Institute of Family Studies[12] and Monash University's five-year research project on the history of adoption in Australia.[13] Numerous publications by both research groups

---

9   This chapter was originally published on 10 December 2020 as a member contribution article without footnotes or references in the Summer 2020 edition of VANISH's newsletter, *Voice*.

10   This figure was reported in the Senate Community Affairs References Committee's report, *Commonwealth Contribution to Former Forced Adoption Policies and Practices* (2012).

11   Ibid.

12   As discussed by Daryl Higgins and Sue Tait in *Request for Feedback and Input on Issues Paper: Establishing an Institute of Open Adoption* (2015).

13   See Marian Quartly, Shirley Swain and Denise Cuthbert's *The Market in Babies: Stories of Australian Adoption* (2013).

highlight that many people have experienced unanticipated consequences from past adoption practices and continue to experience associated harms.

Recognition of the harms led to the formal apologies for historical adoptions made by the federal, state and territory governments from 2010 to 2013. Notwithstanding, the Victorian Government's apology of 2012 by then Premier Ted Baillieu and the national apology of 2013 by then Prime Minister Julia Gillard have so far failed to generate any reform in relation to a major issue for many people adopted in Victoria[14] in the context of pre-1980s policies and practices—namely, legal cancellation of their original birth certificate and erasure of their identity, and replacement with an officially fabricated legal identity and birth certificate. As the Victorian Law Reform Commission's Review of the *Adoption Act 1984* Report noted:

> For many people affected by past closed and forced adoptions, the amended birth certificate symbolises the serious problems they see with adoption ... Their birth certificates represent erasure of their past and fabrication of their birth; a re-writing of their identity ... and dishonesty and injustice which must be corrected.[15]

Since the 1980s, beginning in Victoria with its *Adoption Act 1984*, significant changes have been made to adoption laws across Australia. For new adoptions, these include provisions intended to ensure parents' informed and voluntary consent, and 'openness' through ongoing contact or information exchange between adopted children and their natural families. For past adoptions, the changes include provisions enabling adoptees and other relevant parties to access written records and identifying information about relatives from whom they were separated.

---

14 Indeed, for many people adopted in Australia.
15 Quoted from the Victorian Law Reform Commission's *Review of the Adoption Act 1984: Report* (2017), p. 96.

Some argue this demonstrates Australia has learned from its past mistakes[16] and that contemporary open adoptions differ from and overcome many of the problems of past adoptions.[17] But these arguments overlook the inherently coercive context of adoptions from the statutory child welfare system and the continuing practice of legally fabricating adoptees' birth records and genealogical identities in contemporary open adoptions (and other family formation methods), and continuing impacts of the legal fabrication of adoptees' birth records for those affected by historical adoptions.[18] As argued by Kenny, Higgins and Morley:

> While adoption practices in Australia have undergone considerable change since the 1980s, it is evident that the effects of forced adoption and family separation are still very much a part of the current lived experience for the many thousands of people involved. Further, concerns have been raised that identify the similarities existing between past adoption policies and practices and current child protection policies in some jurisdictions (e.g. permanency planning practices that focus on adoption rather than reunification or long-term out-of-home care) and alternative methods of family formation that are increasingly being used (e.g. inter-country adoption, surrogacy and assisted reproduction technologies).[19]

A consequence of the legal change to their birth certificate and identity for many people adopted during early childhood before

---

16   For example, Damon Martin and Delphine Stadler in 'Promising Practice: Australia's National Apology for Forced Adoptions' (2016).

17   For example, in the report of the House of Representatives Standing Committee on Social Policy and Legal Affairs, *Breaking Barriers: A National Adoption Framework for Australian Children* (2018); and Susan Tregeagle, Elizabeth Cox, Louise Voigt and Lynne Moggach in 'Are We Adequately Considering Children's Rights to a Family?: The Importance of Adoption to Young People in Long-Term Care' (2012).

18   As argued in my PhD thesis, 'The Introduction and Implementation of Permanent Care Orders in Victoria' (2019).

19   Quoted from Pauline Kenny, Daryl J. Higgins and Samuel R. Morley, *Good Practice Principles in Providing Services to Those Affected by Forced Adoption and Family Separation* (2015), p. 1.

the 1980s is that they grew up unaware of their adoption.[20] It is commonplace for adoptees to make this discovery in adulthood, often accidentally, in response to which they can be shocked and their lives dramatically disrupted.[21] In 2016, for example, in NSW, Peter Capomolla Moore inadvertently discovered he was adopted through the results of a consumer genetic genealogy test:

> As the reality dawned on me, I realised everything I thought I'd known about my identity was wrong. The family tree I'd so painstakingly researched for years didn't belong to me at all. Confused and shocked, I felt betrayed by my parents ... Discovering at 59 that I was adopted turned my life upside down.[22]

Despite his shock on discovering his adoption, Capomolla Moore keenly pursued contact with his natural parents and their families.

Those informed early of their adoption can also feel compelled to search for their natural parents. For example, in 2015, in Victoria, Sarah O'Sullivan, who was abandoned as a newborn in 1998 and subsequently adopted by her foster parents, publicly appealed for information about her parents who she had been seeking for some time.[23]

Sarah O'Sullivan may have been delivered alone by her mother outside a hospital environment, possibly with no one else knowing of her pregnancy. In contrast, the more than 45,000 infants formally adopted in Victoria from 1945 to 1975[24] were

---

20 As discussed in the NSW Parliament's Standing Committee on Social Issues report, *Releasing the Past: Adoption Practices 1950–1998, Final Report* (2000); the Senate Community Affairs References Committee's report (2012), Op. cit.; and the Victorian Law Reform Commission's report (2017), Op. cit.

21 See Helen J. Riley's thesis, 'Identity and Genetic Origins: An Ethical Exploration of the Late Discovery of Adoptive and Donor-Insemination Offspring Status' (2012).

22 Quoted from Jessica Bell (2020) 'Adoption Discovery: 59-year-old Man Finds Secret Family', *7news.com.au*.

23 See the article, '"Baby Sophie" Appeals for Parents to Come Forward, 17 Years After Being Dumped in a Public Toilet Block' on *news.com.au* (2015).

24 This figure was reported by Christin Quirk in 'The Business of Adoption: Past Practices at Melbourne's Royal Women's Hospital' (2013).

predominantly born in hospitals, and their mothers had often also spent time beforehand with other young women 'concealing' their ex-nuptial pregnancies in one of the numerous mothers' and babies' homes operated, mostly by church organisations, for that purpose. The mothers were generally not allowed to have a support person with them during labour—now unthinkable, even during the recent COVID-19 crisis,[25] given the many known benefits of this practice.[26]

The largest women's hospitals—the Royal Women's Hospital (RWH) and the Queen Victoria Memorial Hospital (QVMH)—were the most intimately and extensively involved in facilitating the adoption of babies born to unmarried mothers in Victoria.[27] Social workers at the RWH supported early placement of infants for adoption and, as a result, the hospital's nurseries were often filled with newborn babies awaiting placement.[28] A nurse employed at the RWH, as quoted in the Senate Committee's report on the *Commonwealth Contribution to Former Forced Adoption Policies and Practices*, described the practices involved as follows:

> … we had taken babies from their mothers at birth, without them holding or even seeing their child. … The babies stayed in the nurseries in the hospital waiting to be adopted, sometimes for months, their only contact being with the nurses such as myself who cared for them on a daily basis … it wasn't the same as being cared for by their mother.[29]

Attitudes were similar at the QVMH. The photo below shows three nurses at the QVMH tending to at least 20 newborns tucked

---

25 As reported by Rachael Dexter, Paul Sakkal and Simone Koob (24 July 2020), and Kylie Stone (27 July 2020), in *The Age*.

26 See Maria Iliadou's article, 'Supporting Women in Labour' (2012); and Petronellah Lunda, Catharina Minnie and Petronella Benadé's article, 'Women's Experiences of Continuous Support During Childbirth: A Meta-Synthesis' (2018).

27 As noted in the 'History of Queen Victoria Women's Centre' (2019).

28 As reported by Christin Quirk (2013). Op. cit.

29 Senate Community Affairs References Committee (2012). Op. cit., p. 65.

neatly into conjoined cribs—like packages sorted into pigeon-holes, evoking those used for sorting mail in the local post office in eastern Victoria that my late adoptive parents operated from our home from the time I was adopted until I went to university.[30]

Infants in the Queen Victoria Hospital Maternity Ward
Image courtesy of Monash Health Historical Archives Collection

The realisation that hospital maternity wards in Australia were once crammed with babies who were rudely separated from their mothers is now jarring.[31] This is especially so given growing evidence of a range of health and development benefits to mothers

---

30 My late adoptive parents, Lionel and Lois Mackieson, operated the post office at Buchan South for 18 years until its closure in March 1980, as reported in *The Bairnsdale Advertiser* (pp. 6–7) on 31 March 1980.

31 That said, similar images of dozens of babies born through surrogacy trapped in lockdown in Ukraine during the COVID-19 pandemic seem to have engendered more empathy for the commissioning parents than for the surrogate mothers or the babies themselves. See, for example, Mary Ilyushina's article and the accompanying photos on *CNN* (16 May 2020).

and their newborns from maintaining close physical contact with each other and potential harms from not doing so,[32] and increased risk of misidentifying babies in such circumstances.

Internationally, ongoing concern about the potential for accidental and non-accidental baby misidentification in busy maternity wards[33] has generated a specialised field of research on strategies and technologies for its prevention.[34]

In Australia, forensic DNA testing is now available to quickly clarify any suspected cases of baby misidentification in hospitals—unlike in the past.[35] Nevertheless, hospital staff and administrators would be cognisant of the considerable distress and potential repercussions that even a temporary switch of newborns can cause[36]—for example, following an accidental switch of babies in a single breastfeeding incident.[37]

But what about baby misidentifications that occurred prior to the availability of DNA testing? Allegations of poor, unethical and unlawful hospital practices associated with historical adoptions have, understandably, usually been made by mothers whose babies were taken from them.[38] But if the mothers did not get to see or hold their babies, how would they know if their baby was misidentified?

---

32 Some readings on the harms to babies and their mothers from separation after birth are listed in a separate section in the Bibliography.

33 Some readings on international concerns regarding the potential for baby misidentifications in hospitals are listed in a separate section in the Bibliography.

34 Some readings on the specialist research for prevention of baby misidentification are listed in a separate section in the Bibliography.

35 For contrast, see Crispin Hull's discussion of unusual and interesting cases in the High Court of Australia from 1903–2003 (c. 2003).

36 For example, as reported by Adam Cooper (18 July 2011); and analysed by Tara Crane (2000), and Marc D. Ginsberg (2010).

37 See the articles by Tess Koman (21 January 2016); Emer McLysaght (2011); James Robertson (21 January 2016); and Charles W. Sauer and Krishelle L. Marc-Aurele (2016).

38 For example, see Jewel Topsfield's article, "'It walks with you forever': Mothers sue hospital that took their babies', in *The Age* (27 December 2019).

Peter Capomolla Moore's story shows how consumer genetic genealogy testing can inadvertently reveal the historical secret of their adoption to an adoptee.

Consumer genetic genealogy testing can also inadvertently reveal another secret to an adoptee—even an adoptee who has always known of their adoption. Years after having accessed their official adoption records, and successfully searched for and established long-term relationships with their 'natural' family, consumer genetic genealogy testing can reveal to an adoptee that they were misidentified as a newborn baby in hospital prior to their adoptive placement. In other words, the original birth certificate issued to them when they applied for their records was not actually theirs, and their reunion of more than 20 years was with the wrong mother and family.

This is what happened to me.

CHAPTER 2

Through the DNA Looking Glass

"Apparently, I physically resemble my father's side of my family more closely than [my mother's]." That's what I wrote on page 18 of *Adoption Deception* because that's what I was firmly led to believe from 1990 when I accessed my official adoption records. It's also what was reinforced to me from 1997 when I first reached out to Gwen,[39] my mother—that is, my natural mother as identified in my official adoption records. As was common in 1963 in relation to babies born to single mothers, Gwen disclosed no information to the authorities about my father's identity during her pregnancy or when she registered my birth. Nor did Gwen tell my father about her pregnancy with me. When Gwen told me that, I realised my father would never come looking for me. If I wanted to contact him, which I most certainly did, I was totally reliant on Gwen to provide information about him because there was no other way to obtain it. Consumer genetic genealogy testing wasn't a thing in 1990 or even in 1997.[40]

---

39 "Gwen" is an alias first name.

40 See the International Society of Genetic Genealogy Wiki (2018) for information about genetic genealogy.

Gwen told me that I looked more like my father's family in relation to my dark colouring, presumably in reference to my brown hair and brown eyes given my skin is naturally pale. Gwen said this in response to my disappointment after viewing her family photo albums because I felt I didn't especially resemble her or any other members of her family at any stage of my life. Indeed, to me my face looked more like my adoptive mother's than my natural mother's. By then I'd met or seen photos of all my maternal half-siblings and had also seen photos of members of Gwen's extended family. I wrote "apparently" in *Adoption Deception* because up to that time I'd never seen any evidence of my purported resemblance to my father's family. I didn't get to meet my father, aside from a single phone conversation with him that was facilitated by Gwen, only a few weeks before he died unexpectedly. Nor had I met any of his siblings or his other children who he told me about, nor seen any photos of him or them. Frankly, it gnawed at me.

I desperately wanted to see a clear family resemblance to someone naturally related to me, preferably a member or members of my maternal family who I already knew and loved. But no matter how hard I wished it, I simply couldn't see it. Some in my closest social network believed they did see a physical resemblance between me and my sister, Kylie,[41] the maternal half-sibling to whom I was socially closest. They variously identified that we have similar eyes, despite mine being more open-set and upward tilting at the outside corners compared with Kylie's; or similar hand gestures, despite that my hands are square with short fingers whereas Kylie's hands and fingers are so nicely shaped and proportioned that she could be a hand model; or similarly pronounce certain words, which is probably more an observation of how we slur our speech a little after one too many glasses of pinot gris. One friend even saw a similarity I'd never discerned between my nondescript handwriting

---

41 "Kylie" is an alias first name.

16

and Gwen's much neater and more stylish but slightly backward-leaning script.

Anyway, on turning 50, I was perturbed at being so far into my life without having met any natural relative whose face—or body, mannerisms, personality, interests or talents, for that matter—mirrored my own. "Family faces are magic mirrors. Looking at people who belong to us, we see the past, present, and future."[42] The previous statement is about genetic mirroring[43] and, while true for everyone, it has particular importance for adopted individuals: "In the empty genetic mirror the adoptee stands alone."[44] Genetically alone is exactly how I felt, despite having had years of social contact with Gwen and my maternal half-siblings. Actually, apart from some tiny details in relation to our ears, knees and elbows, I barely even saw myself physically reflected in my son, Patrick.

The dissonance in my feelings relating to family resemblance and belonging motivated me to reach out to my paternal family. This included formally applying to VANISH's search service for assistance in identifying and locating close relatives of my late father with a view to obtaining photos of him, his other children and/or his siblings. VANISH was able to identify one of my paternal aunts and provided me with guidance in regard to contacting her directly, just as they did in 1997 when I reached out to Gwen. I wrote a very brief letter to my aunt indicating that I was searching for a person by her name and born to parents I also named (knowing they were my father's parents), and requested that she contact me. My aunt responded promptly via phone and was understandably surprised, but friendly, when I explained who I was and the reason for my

---

42 Attributed to Gail L. Buckley, as quoted by Andi Willis in 'Inspiring Quotes About Family and Family History' (2020).

43 See Jeanette Yoffe (2021) 'Genetic Mirroring: What It Is, How It Affects Adopted People, and What You Can Do About It'.

44 I saw this quotation on a website for 'Adoption Birth Mothers' in 2022 but have been unable to locate the website since.

contact. She seemed to engage and agreed to send me photos of my father. However, I never received any photos, nor any response to my subsequent voicemail messages and second letter. I was very disappointed but felt I had to leave it at that.

I employed another, far less direct, approach by taking an AncestryDNA test in 2016. A good friend, Pauline Ley OAM,[45] who was also adopted in Australia, successfully connected with paternal relatives overseas through consumer genetic genealogy testing, albeit that it took several years and a generous genetic genealogist's patient assistance. In discussions with Pauline I concluded there was nothing to lose by taking an AncestryDNA test. At the time it rather felt like an improbable last-ditch effort to connect with my paternal family members. But it also felt like planting a seed that could germinate and bear fruit at some unknown time in the future. Obviously, the results depended on at least one other person reasonably closely related to me having also taken an AncestryDNA test. But I was aware that consumer genetic genealogy testing was becoming increasingly popular,[46] just as online genealogy tracing websites were already popular worldwide because the human "need to trace one's roots is not limited to adoptees in search of living blood relatives."[47] From my single phone contact with my father I was also aware that I had several paternal half-siblings, so I was hopeful that one of them or their children may have done the test or would do so in the not-too-distant future.

While I waited for notification about my AncestryDNA test results, I tried to be realistic and not get my hopes up again. But as we all know, that is often much easier said than done. At least I was fully occupied and could distract myself with my PhD studies,

---

45   See VANISH's article, 'VANISH Founding Member Honoured in Queen's Birthday Awards', in the Winter 2018 edition of *Voice*.
46   See Anthony Regalado (12 February 2018) '2017 Was the Year Consumer DNA Testing Blew Up'.
47   Quoted from Mike Chalek and Jessica Gardner (2012). Op. cit., p. 57.

which I'd been undertaking for about a year by that stage. I kept my head busy with the stuff I did best—study—because I knew it could provide comfort irrespective of the outcome of my AncestryDNA test. But when the test results arrived some six or so weeks later, my overriding reaction was puzzlement.

When I logged in to my Ancestry account I navigated directly to the 'DNA Relatives' page. I was immediately disappointed that the closest matches were distant, no closer than fourth to sixth cousins. Next I felt full on confusion. Not only were none of the names of the people listed as my DNA matches even remotely familiar to me but at least half were Greek, very Greek. It simply didn't make sense. So I then navigated to the 'DNA Story' page, which displayed a list of estimated percentages for each ethnicity making up my DNA heritage and a world map depicting, with different coloured shading, the geographical region for each of those ethnicities. The information displayed there made me even more perplexed. I saw no percentages for Wales, England or Ireland and had to click on a drop-down box. It said zero per cent for all the countries of the British Isles. Instead, my listed ethnicities indicated 69% for Greece and the Balkans, 15% for Turkey and the Caucasus, 9% for Italy, 5% for Eastern Europe and Russia, and 2% for Southern Asia. My largest ethnicity percentage was denoted by a dotted line around the shaded area on the world map for Greece. Yep, Greece!

My mind raced. I remembered often having wondered as a child, teenager and young adult whether my natural parents— my natural mother, at least—had Greek, Italian or some other European ancestry. This was because my late adoptive parents had always maintained that the QVMH social worker who handed me over to them said my mother was from an inner northern suburb of Melbourne, an area I knew to be very multicultural even when I was a child living in a small rural town in eastern Victoria. It seemed quite plausible that I had European heritage early in my social work career, too. I worked in the western suburbs of

Melbourne and people from various European ethnic backgrounds would often start speaking to me in their first language. They simply assumed that I shared their cultural heritage, that I was one of them. In that context, on several occasions I was told that I resembled the respective speaker's cousin. This reinforced a feeling I had growing up that I resembled everyone a little but no one in particular. Regardless, thoughts of possibly having a European background were snuffed out in 1990 when I obtained my adoption records because they pointed to Anglo-Celtic heritage.[48] But now, decades on, did I really have evidence that my ancestry is Greek after all?

It was too soon to be getting excited or panicked. I needed to remain calm and deal with this unexpected information rationally. No doubt there would be a perfectly good explanation for my DNA test results. For instance, the lab may have mixed up my saliva sample. Indeed, that was the most obvious possibility. The first thing I needed to do was check that out, and so I did. I emailed Ancestry explaining that, although I was adopted, I had obtained my official adoption records with my natural mother's identifying details; had subsequently established a relationship with her and knew that she had Welsh-English heritage; and had obtained identifying information from her about my late putative father who I believed was of Irish-English heritage. On the basis that my test results showed no Celtic-Anglo ethnicity at all and overwhelmingly Greek ethnicity instead, I requested that Ancestry check whether my sample had been misidentified. Ancestry's prompt reply indicated it is not uncommon for people to be surprised (surely a euphemism for *shocked!*) by their DNA test results, and reminded me this was a risk I'd accepted when I authorised them to analyse my saliva sample. Ancestry assured me that my sample had been

---

48   As discussed in *Adoption Deception* (2015). Op. cit., pp. 11–12.

correctly identified. So, the most obvious explanation for my unexpected DNA test results was eliminated.

Until then I hadn't let myself think too much about it, although I'd probably been holding my breath, metaphorically speaking. But now I felt uneasy. The percentage of Greek ethnicity indicated in my test results was way more than 50%. I'm no geneticist but, from my high school biology and undergraduate psychology classes, I realised that even if one of my parents was 100% Greek (which was extraordinarily unlikely), I could inherit no more than 50% of my Greek ethnicity from that particular parent. In other words, my AncestryDNA test results indicated that both my parents were of Greek heritage.

Gwen knew very well that I'd sought contact with my father before he died. However, I hadn't informed Gwen or any of her other children that I was trying to connect with my natural paternal relatives or that I'd taken an AncestryDNA test for that purpose. I was a mature adult. I didn't need their permission and hadn't sought it. Still, I began to stress about discussing the matter with them, anticipating that it probably wouldn't go down well. From various conversations over the years with Kylie, in particular, I gathered that she didn't like discussing Gwen's life before she met and married Kylie's father. But I knew I couldn't avoid addressing the matter; that I'd have to tell Gwen I'd taken an AncestryDNA test as context for seeking an explanation for the puzzling results. To me, this was the obvious next step in working it out. I needed to check whether Gwen knew for sure that she was the natural daughter of the parents who raised her, whether she may also have been adopted and have Greek heritage; and whether any other man could be my father apart from the one she identified to me, and whether he could also have Greek heritage.

I first raised the matter with Gwen in December 2016. Kylie was there, too, as was our usual routine when Bruce, Patrick and I visited. I remember it clearly because I'd spent much time beforehand worrying about raising the matter and psyching myself up for it. During the visit I agonised over finding an appropriate segue in the conversation—something to do with surprises, if I recall correctly—to mention that I'd taken an AncestryDNA test. Before relaying the results I explained that I'd already contacted Ancestry and confirmed my sample had not been mixed up in their lab.

It appeared from the beginning that neither Gwen nor Kylie set much store by consumer genetic genealogy tests in general, and in my AncestryDNA test results in particular. Gwen seemed amused and related stories of the Greek people she'd known growing up, making clear in the process that she'd never gone out with a man of Greek heritage. The conversation quickly got awkward, however, when I ventured to explore with Gwen her confidence in the facts of her own paternity and of mine. It wasn't so much what was said as what wasn't said. I read Gwen and Kylie's sidelong glances at each other and, especially, their intermittent eyebrow raising and eye rolling to mean they were both sceptical of my concern. I gained the distinct impression that neither were about to volunteer to take a DNA test to clarify our genetic relationships. I very much wanted to know the truth of my ancestry. But not at the cost of my longstanding positive relationships with my maternal family, especially Gwen and Kylie. It felt far too fraught to ask them outright. This was frustrating, as well as disappointing, even if I'd predicted such a response as the worst-case scenario.

Nevertheless, during the course of the conversation, Kylie disclosed that she'd compiled a family tree on Ancestry for each side of her family dating back several generations and that she'd be happy to give me full access to her maternal family tree. It was comforting to know that Kylie considered me a full member of her family based on the official documents I'd accessed years prior, even if it still nagged at me that I didn't share a close family resemblance. But I was also surprised and bemused. In all the years we'd known each other and in all the time we'd spent together, including trips overseas, Kylie had never mentioned that she used Ancestry. I felt I'd always been very open with her about the importance to me of knowing my genealogical roots—after all, that's why I'd reached out to Gwen in the first place. But Kylie hadn't shared with me the extent of her interest in her own genealogical roots. On the one hand Kylie implicitly trusted the document trail relating to her genealogy but on the other she didn't seem to trust the DNA evidence relating to mine. I found it curious. Still, I took up Kylie's invitation and accessed the maternal family tree on Ancestry. It was exactly as Kylie had described, with deep continuous roots in Wales and England. It included an entry for each of my maternal half-siblings and their partners and children, as appropriate. As there were no entries for me, Bruce and Patrick, I added them.

Thereafter I tried not to think too much about my puzzling AncestryDNA test results and to stay focused on my PhD. But it bubbled away in the back of my mind and, when I relaxed, too often also in the front of my mind. I couldn't help but raise the matter in some further conversations with Gwen and Kylie. I never got past first base with Gwen. She would repeat the stories she'd shared during that first conversation about the Greek people she knew growing up. This meant she had nothing further to add and effectively signalled the end of the discussion. It reminded me of conversations with Mum (my late adoptive mother) when I was growing up in relation to whether I might search for my natural mother in the future. Mum would repeat the story of my handover at three weeks of age at the QVMH and the limited information the social worker told her and Dad about my natural mother. That also signalled it was all Mum considered relevant and thus the end of the discussion.

I didn't even get to first base with Kylie. I clearly recall three very uncomfortable conversations with her—or more accurately, in her presence. One was while dining with a group of girlfriends on a trip overseas, another was while dining out in Melbourne with friends planning another trip overseas, and the other was during pre-dinner drinks one evening with Kylie and her close girlfriends. On each occasion Kylie completely clammed up—her facial expression and body froze and, staring straight ahead, she said absolutely nothing, not a word, until the conversation moved on to another topic. In a masterful display of passive aggression, Kylie always seemed totally fine with me afterward, as if the topic of my AncestryDNA test results had never been mentioned at all. Nevertheless, from hearing those discussions, Kylie should have understood that a close family member taking a DNA test would help clarify our genetic relationships and solve my DNA puzzle. Yet without uttering a single word, Kylie reinforced the accuracy of my reading of her from the first time I raised the matter—that she was not only unwilling to take such a test but would also refuse if I asked her outright. I was too afraid to ask either Kylie or Gwen for fear of negative impact on our relationships. Yet I also knew that, at some stage, I would have to deal with this most primal of matters concerning my identity to which I'd devoted most of my adulthood.

Meanwhile, completing my PhD was not without its own dramas. The biggest of those disrupted my plan for the second of two research projects: the first project was qualitative and the other was to be quantitative. The quantitative research project aimed to analyse anonymised administrative data routinely collected by DHHS in the context of its child protection and out-of-home care programs for the period from 1 January 1995 to 31 December 2016, inclusive. The purpose was to explore how the implementation of Permanent Care Orders (PCOs) had addressed the issues that led to their introduction in the first place. In conjunction with my two PhD supervisors from the University of Melbourne's Social Work Department, Professor Marie Connolly (my primary supervisor, and Chair and Head of the Department) and Professor

Aron Shlonsky,[49] we made successful applications to DHHS and the relevant ethics committee to access the data. We initiated the research project in February 2017 and received approval from DHHS's Centre for Evaluation and Research on 21 September the same year. But there was a catch.

The letter of approval also advised of "a new requirement" for DHHS's Centre for Evaluation and Research "to advise the Minister for Families and Children of all requests for release of out of home care data." This process was expected to take a further six to eight weeks. By January 2018, we had anticipated not only having been able to access the data but possibly also having completed the statistical analyses, particularly because there had been no indication from DHHS of any issues with our application. But there was still no word from DHHS, meaning they'd had no word from the Minister's Office, and we couldn't wait indefinitely if I was to complete my PhD in a timely manner. So we decided to move on to an alternative means of exploring the implementation of PCOs in Victoria and, early in February 2018, sent a letter to DHHS explaining this and formally withdrawing our data request.

The letters must have crossed in the post because the next day I received a letter from DHHS advising they were now "unable to support [my] individual research application because this area of research will be covered by the longitudinal research in response to the Commission's [i.e. CCYP's] recommendation."[50] Really? My research project aimed to explore PCOs from when they commenced operation in 1992, although on DHHS's advice this was amended to 1995 because the data was apparently unreliable before

---

49 Professor Shlonsky has been Head of the Social Work Department at Monash University since late 2018.

50 This refers to Recommendation 40 of the Commission for Children and Young People's *Safe and Wanted* report (2017, p. 34) to undertake "a longitudinal study of children subject to child protection involvement after March 2016 to monitor and track outcomes for these children and determine whether or not the permanency amendments are achieving their objectives."

then. However, the CCYP-recommended research project aimed to explore PCO outcomes from when the permanency amendments commenced operation in March 2016. This meant there was only a ten-month period of overlap (from March to December 2016, inclusive) of the data sought for my PhD research project (which spanned over 20 years) with the data to be analysed by the CCYP-recommended research project. Had it been requested, I would most willingly have brought forward the end date relating to my data request to February 2016, thereby eliminating any data overlap whatsoever in the two research projects. That I was not consulted about it by the Minister's Office or DHHS suggested there was an ulterior motive.

Reading between the bureaucratese, the new requirement to "advise" the Minister seemed to indicate that a Ministerial approval process had been added to an existing bureaucratic approval process in an apparently arbitrary exercise of control by either the Minister or the Minister's advisory staff.[51] The Minister and I had had some contact before my PhD research in the context of my advocacy work in relation to adoption. This included the Victorian Government's election campaign commitment to extend eligibility to adopt to same-sex couples, as discussed in *Adoption Deception*,[52] because of my concerns that expanding such eligibility would fuel increased demand in Victoria for children to adopt and further undermine much-needed discourse on whether adoptions should be done at all in the state. I wondered whether as a result of that advocacy I had been wrongly labelled by the Minister's Office as 'anti-gay', given the Victorian Government's championing of 'LGBTIQ+' interests.[53] Was I being paranoid? Could the Minister's

---

51 See Shannon Deery's article, 'State's Integrity Deficit: Watchdog Warns on "Soft Corruption"' (22 October 2022).

52 See pp. 89–92.

53 See the Victorian Government's *Pride in Our Future: Victoria's LGBTIQ+ Strategy 2022–32* (2022).

Office have deliberately introduced the extra approval process to stall release of the data for my PhD project so they had time to devise a plausible excuse to overturn DHHS's approval? Could they have instructed DHHS to find a way to deny my data request, no matter how tenuous? I was well aware of the role of Ministerial staffers,[54] that they control "much communication between a department and its minister ... They decide what's too trivial, inconvenient or potentially embarrassing to be passed on"[55] and, as a consequence, that "government decisions may not be made on merit, but pushed into more partisan or political considerations."[56] Irrespective of any assessment of my data application by the Minister's staff, the timing of the CCYP's *Safe and Wanted* report could not have been more convenient for them. That report was submitted to the Minister in June 2017 and publicly released by the Minister in December 2017. Whatever. It was a process that was beyond my control.

Meanwhile, I invested the time during the waiting period in processes that were within my control. I undertook several online courses on research methodologies and statistical analyses and, on the suggestion of the chair of my four-person PhD supervisory panel,[57] prepared an article on the methodology I'd used for my (first) qualitative research project. The article, titled 'Increasing rigor and reducing bias in qualitative research: A document analysis of parliamentary debates using applied thematic analysis', was published by the international *Qualitative Social Work* journal,

---

54 See, for example, Margaret Simons' article, 'The Daniel Andrews Paradox: The Enduring Appeal of Australia's Most Divisive Premier' (30 October 2022).
55 Quoted from Ross Gittins (30 September 2020) 'If You Do Health Admin on the Cheap, Don't Be Amazed If Things Go Wrong'.
56 Quoted from Chip Le Grand and Paul Sakkal (5 November 2022) 'IBAC Probe Uncovers a Troubling Picture'.
57 The Chair of my PhD supervisory panel was Professor Lynette Joubert, and the fourth member was Dr Trish McNamara.

first online in 2018 and subsequently in print the following year.[58] According to the relevant metrics, that article is frequently read and widely cited and has generated significantly more academic interest than the other three articles and thesis from my PhD research combined. So on a positive note, if not for the unnecessary Ministerial delay that ended in the questionable overturning of DHHS's approval for my data application, I may not have written that article at all.

Late in 2018 I could see the finish line for my PhD. Despite the pivot required after having to drop my planned quantitative research project, I managed to complete a second qualitative research project and was making good progress on my thesis. I was on track to submit it by the end of January 2019 and my thoughts began drifting more frequently to sorting out my DNA dilemma. I was beginning to grapple with the possibility that there had, indeed, been a misidentification. But given the confirmation by Ancestry that there had not been a lab mix-up with my saliva sample, I had to consider that it might actually be *me* who'd been misidentified as a newborn baby at the QVMH. I ran this theory past some social worker friends and colleagues with extensive experience in child protection and adoption matters and noted some scepticism, especially by those who saw a resemblance between me and Kylie. Nevertheless, in conversation with Bruce one evening while we were out for dinner together, he reflected that this issue would consume me if I didn't resolve it, which he strongly encouraged me to do sooner rather than later. I agreed with him but still felt the need to tread cautiously.

So I decided to take another consumer genetic genealogy test, this time with 23andMe, to confirm the reliability of my Ancestry-DNA test. The results were strikingly similar. The 23andMe test

---

58   See Penny Mackieson, Aron Shlonsky and Marie Connolly (2019). 'Increasing Rigor and Reducing Bias in Qualitative Research: A Document Analysis of Parliamentary Debates Using Applied Thematic Analysis'.

results even provided further information that strongly suggested both sides of my family were from a particular region of mainland Greece. Wow! Next I decided to ask Bruce and Patrick to each take an AncestryDNA test. Their results arrived in early 2019 and, as we expected, clearly and correctly identified that I'm Patrick's mother, Bruce is Patrick's father and, reciprocally, that Patrick is Bruce's and my son. Patrick's test results showed that his biggest percentage of ethnic heritage (almost 40%) originates from Greece and the Balkans—that is, from me. The composition of my own ethnic heritage had been adjusted to 82% for Greece and the Balkans, up from the original 69% since my AncestryDNA test in 2016, following the upload of tens of thousands of additional test results to the database in the intervening period. Bruce's ethnicity results confirmed, as we expected, that his family origins are predominantly from England, Wales and Northwestern Europe (63%) and Ireland and Scotland (33%), similar to what we'd originally expected mine to be. Even more helpful, though, Bruce recognised the names of several cousins from both sides of his family on his 'DNA Relatives' page whose relationships to him were identified correctly according to his pre-existing knowledge of his family tree. It was an aside, though still a relief, that Bruce's test results also confirmed he and I are not genetically related, as I'd always feared accidentally partnering with someone closely related to me.[59] Our combined results confirmed the power of AncestryDNA testing and emboldened me to take the next step in addressing the puzzle of my parentage.

It seemed inevitable that I would have to ask Gwen to take a DNA test, too. While mustering the courage, I decided to have another crack at accessing my QVMH records. Despite Monash Health's response to my first FOI application in 2014 indicating

---

59   As discussed in *Adoption Deception* (2015). Op. cit., pp. 5–6.

that my QVMH records had likely been destroyed,[60] I understood through my involvement in the Victorian adoption community that other individuals who were born at the QVMH and subsequently adopted around the same time I was had been successful in gaining access to their QVMH records. This was another thing that simply didn't make sense to me. I knew it was a long shot but figured that if my records hadn't actually been destroyed, if they'd been mislaid and could be located, they might provide valuable clues regarding what happened to me while I was in hospital and obviate the need to ask Gwen to take a DNA test after all. To this end, in March 2019 I submitted a second FOI application to Monash Health seeking records relating to my birth and three-week period at the QVMH in 1963 before my placement for adoption. My application outlined the results of my consumer genetic genealogy tests and explained that I was weighing up whether to risk the social relationship I'd developed with Gwen since 1997 by asking her to do a DNA test to clarify our genetic relationship. The reply from Monash Health arrived early in April 2019, reiterating that they were unable to locate any medical records relating to me or my mother. I knew that I really did need to muster my courage now.

A week or so later I bit the bullet and asked Gwen to take an AncestryDNA test. In isolation, the decision to do so was easy because it was logical. What was not easy, however, was how to go about asking her. I mulled over simply jumping in the car and driving the 150 kilometres to her house mid-week unannounced, as I'd already purchased an AncestryDNA test kit for her. But I'd almost always phoned beforehand to check that she'd be home and that it was convenient for her when planning to visit, which was usually on a weekend. This meant that Kylie, who lived near Gwen, would generally also be able to join us. However, this time I didn't want Kylie to be present because I feared she would

---

60   Ibid, pp. 136–137.

actively discourage Gwen from taking the test. Yet nor did I want to ambush Gwen, either by visiting unexpectedly or by the influence of my personality when we were alone together—that would not have been fair. The clash between the need for Gwen to have both time and space to consider my request and my increasingly urgent need to clarify my parentage was almost paralysing.

I discussed it further with Bruce who remained keen for me to get on with it. Ultimately I decided the best way to proceed was to phone Gwen, which I did. I emphasised to her the importance to me of resolving the puzzle of my 2016 AncestryDNA test results and informed her of the results of the further consumer genetic genealogy tests that Bruce, Patrick and I had taken. I also explained how her taking an AncestryDNA test would clarify whether or not we had a genetic mother-daughter relationship. Without further ado, and catching me quite by surprise, Gwen agreed to do the test. After so much anxiety for so long about asking her, it was an enormous relief. Then for the same reason I'd decided to phone Gwen rather than visit in person, I also decided to post the test kit to her—to ensure she had space to change her mind if she so wished on further consideration. Of course, I remained anxious that Kylie would try to talk her out of it or simply refuse to register the test. Gwen was not familiar with using computers and, when I explained to her that her sample would need to be registered online before being posted to the lab, she advised she would ask Kylie to do it rather than send the sample back to me for this purpose. Fair enough. It was Gwen's DNA sample and her decision. I could do nothing further for the time being except wait … impatiently.

Gwen agreed to let me know the results of her AncestryDNA test when she received them. I'd requested this because I realised I wouldn't be alerted through my Ancestry account should those results indicate we were not genetically related, and I was most anxious to learn the results. So, aware there was an approximately two-week processing period for AncestryDNA test results at the time, I phoned Gwen a fortnight after I figured her sample would have arrived at the lab. If Gwen had already received her results, not only did she not mention it during our brief phone call, but she didn't even confirm that she'd taken the test. Gwen ended the call abruptly, before I had an opportunity to ask about her test results, apparently when there was nothing further she wished to say to me. Already there seemed to be fallout from me having asked Gwen to do the test.

The wait was almost unbearable. Somehow I managed to hold on for another week before phoning Gwen again. Once more she didn't mention her AncestryDNA test or the results. So, once again I had to bite the bullet. I asked Gwen directly whether she'd received notification yet. She replied, "Yes." A long pregnant pause followed. She offered no further details. So, I took a deep breath then asked about her DNA matches and ethnicity results. Gwen replied that her ethnicity results were predominantly Welsh and English, which we agreed was completely consistent with the maternal family tree compiled by Kylie on Ancestry. I then asked whether she had any Greek ethnicity. Gwen replied that she had none, zero per cent. Curiously, Gwen then shared that Kylie had already received an email outreach from a not-too-distant cousin in the UK and that they had confirmed each other's position on their respective family trees. I interpreted this as providing evidence to Kylie and Gwen regarding the power and accuracy of AncestryDNA testing. But still Gwen offered no information about her genetic relationship to me. This must have meant my name had not appeared on her 'DNA Relatives' list, given no reciprocal entry for her had appeared on mine. But to be absolutely sure, I asked.

The answer was extremely disappointing. But it was not unexpected—at least by me. I had tried to bring Gwen's understanding of the gravity of my AncestryDNA test results along with me from soon after I received them in 2016. But I had clearly failed. Gwen never seemed to grasp it. I could only imagine her feelings now that the 'penny' had finally dropped for her, now that she realised I was not in fact the first child to whom she gave birth. How much Gwen would have heard or even wanted to hear at that time, I don't know. I endeavoured to acknowledge her shock and express empathy but Gwen didn't say much back. I wasn't sure what else to say but felt obliged to gently step her through the implications. I reiterated that the primary purpose of Gwen having taken the AncestryDNA test was to check whether we were genetically related; that now we had clear evidence we were not related; that I must have been misidentified as her baby in hospital prior to my adoptive placement; and that this meant her real natural daughter was out there somewhere.

I informed Gwen that I intended to contact the Victorian Government's Adoption Information Service (AIS) to try and discover the identity of my real natural mother, who must be Greek, and that Gwen could do the same if she wished to try and discover the identity of her real natural daughter. I also requested that Gwen forward me a copy of her AncestryDNA results so that I could provide it as evidence to AIS, to which she agreed before abruptly ending our conversation. I couldn't help but wonder if she'd already known the results of her AncestryDNA test when I phoned the week before but couldn't bring herself to tell me then.

I'd gone through the DNA looking glass and was now in unfamiliar territory. All I knew for sure was that there was no way back, no way to put the discovery of my heritage and mis-identification back. But I didn't want to put it back. Denial wouldn't have changed the facts. As once famously said by former New York Senator, Daniel Patrick Moynihan, "Everyone is entitled to his own opinions, but not his own facts."[61] The facts were the facts, regardless of what I or anyone else thought about them, regardless of what I or anyone else felt about them. Having Greek parentage

---

61   Quoted from BrainyQuote (2001–2022) 'Daniel Patrick Moynihan Quotes'.

and being genetically unrelated to the family I was officially led to believe was my natural maternal family were not my subjective facts, rather they were *the facts*, the truth of the situation. There was nothing to be gained from denying those facts unless one wished to be complicit in the perpetuation of another appalling adoption deception.

Intellectually, I knew it was reasonable to ask questions about my heritage and seek the answers; that this sorry mess was not of my doing. But I also knew that the truth can be most inconvenient and painful, especially when delivered by an adopted person. Emotionally, I felt some would probably still blame me for what I'd discovered, accuse me of wrecking family relationships, of being ungrateful for what I already had. Fresh in my mind was an experience that happened to me in 2016, before I began to discover I must have been misidentified prior to my adoptive placement. A review of *Adoption Deception* published in an Australian child welfare journal suggested I should be more grateful for my adoption.[62] I had not intended *Adoption Deception* to be an academic treatment of adoption,[63] nevertheless the reviewers chose to critique the book as if it were. Whether or not that treatment was intentional, the critique undermined the validity of my personal experience of adoption—a classic adoption microaggression.[64] The critique was hurtful because, as I shared in *Adoption Deception*, I've always been very grateful for the love, care and opportunities that my adoptive parents gave me.[65] Even so, I also resent being expected to preface every comment I make about my adoption with statements idolising my adoptive parents, adoptive family

---

62 Refer to Susan Tregeagle and Deirdre Cheers (2016) 'Searching for Truths in the Debate About Adoption From Care'.

63 Indeed, I even wrote *Adoption Deception* before I commenced my PhD studies in August 2015.

64 See Amanda Baden's article, '"Do You Know Your Real Parents?" and Other Adoption Microaggressions' (2016).

65 See *Adoption Deception* (2015). Op. cit., p. 13.

relationships or adoptive upbringing, as if I should also be grateful for having been forcibly separated from my mother at birth and stripped of my rightful identity.

While I felt relieved to have clarified my immediate DNA puzzle, I also felt unmoored and in need of answers to many more questions. Who am I? Who are my natural parents? Did they marry each other or someone else? Are my parents still alive? If so, where are they? Do I have any full siblings or half-siblings? Do I resemble any genetic relatives? Was my misidentification accidental or deliberate? Was my identity swapped directly with another baby's or were there more misidentifications and baby swaps involved? How can I find out, given the apparent destruction of my QVMH records? What should I do next?

Of course, I would contact AIS as I'd told Gwen I intended to do. But in the meantime, what if Gwen's eldest daughter was searching for her mother via AncestryDNA? I appreciated exactly how bewildered and frustrated she might feel if she found a close DNA match with Gwen but then also found an imposter—*me!*—with the same birth date and adopted status as herself on the maternal family tree. I had no wish to inflict on anyone else the sort of angst I'd experienced in unravelling my parentage puzzle, so I hastened to remove the entries I'd added for me, Bruce and Patrick from Kylie's maternal family tree on Ancestry. Unfortunately, my instinct to correct those records as soon as possible may have been the last straw in triggering Kylie's blame response.

Kylie emailed me a screen shot of Gwen's AncestryDNA ethnicity results within a few days of me having requested them and took the opportunity to unleash an emotional tirade. I empathised with Kylie's hurt about discovering after so many years that we are not related. Nevertheless, I was deeply upset by her wrong assumptions about my motivation for taking the AncestryDNA test in the first place, her unkind accusations about the way in which I asked Gwen to also take an AncestryDNA test, and her subsequent anger toward me. It was some six weeks before I was able to regain enough composure to reply courteously. I replied in a deliberately formal manner, focusing on the facts and keeping my own emotional responses in check. I sought to avoid expressing something in the moment in writing that I might regret later. In her next email to me, Kylie criticised me for that, too, having apparently perceived my words as cold and uncaring. From my perspective, Kylie had acted like an ostrich, burying her head in the sand whenever I'd raised the issue of the puzzling results from my AncestryDNA test. Kylie had made clear she did not wish to hear the questions I was asking or contemplate their potential implications, let alone help me find the answers. Now that there was a decisive answer, Kylie didn't like it. Perhaps she distrusted it, she certainly blamed me for it and criticised me for how I went about clarifying it. It seemed to me that Kylie found it easier to shoot the messenger, especially via email, than face the facts. In my next email reply to her I indicated that I wasn't prepared to engage in an argument via email and that I preferred to speak with her via phone or in person when she was ready to discuss the matter. Sadly, it appears Kylie may never be ready to have that conversation with me. At the time of writing, it had been four years since my last email to Kylie (in July 2019) and I had still received no response from her. We've both had to grieve the loss of our sisterly relationship, but I will always treasure the many good times and fun we had together.

Meanwhile I maintained contact with Gwen, making phone calls to her as well as sending cards and flowers on significant dates. Gwen's responses, however, were briefer and more formal than before she took the AncestryDNA test to such an extent that I felt too uncomfortable to visit her, not until she thawed. I became increasingly less comfortable about phoning her, too, as she'd become quite terse, keeping our phone calls short and ending them abruptly. Gwen didn't phone me at all, so the frequency of our phone conversations dropped away. Eventually, in February 2020, I received a card, ostensibly in response to the flowers I'd recently sent her. The front of the card was warm and welcoming, featuring a pretty floral design and 'Thank you' written in a large attractive font. But it was a deception. As I flipped the front cover I immediately noticed that Gwen's handwriting was smaller and neater than usual and that her note began low on the inside of the front cover, as if she'd practised it for fit before transcribing the final version onto the inside of the card. The message expressed that the past year had been very difficult for Gwen and her family; that my outreaches to her were distressing; and then the final blow, that she and her family had to move on with their lives. So, just like that, after more than 20 years of relationships, Gwen and her family had decided to move on without me, Bruce and Patrick in their lives. The glass-half-full part of me viewed the card as an expression of Gwen's appreciation, not just for the flowers but also for our mutually loving relationships over the years, and a reluctant farewell. But the glass-half-empty part of me viewed the card more straightforwardly as a polite begone.

Gwen's comment that my outreaches to her were distressing seemed loaded, though I'm still unsure what she meant. At the time, I interpreted it as implying that she blamed me for the ending of our relationships and, perhaps, even that she considered I was taunting her, rubbing salt into her wounds. This fits with a shadow narrative—a shame narrative—long evident to me that the adopted person is often held responsible for how other parties to their adoption feel because the adopted person is also, albeit unreasonably, held responsible for the 'shameful' misfortune of having been conceived and born outside marriage in the first place. Adults' feelings are projected onto an adopted infant and a child's voice can easily be ignored. But it takes much more effort to suppress an adopted person's voice once they've grown into adulthood. Little wonder that adoption legislation continues to treat the adopted person as an 'adopted child', irrespective of their age—to maintain the suppression of their voice. Such treatment is emblematic of the wider societal undermining and silencing of adopted persons' voices, as I've experienced across key domains of my life. Professionally, such as in 2016, when the critique of *Adoption Deception* was published in an Australian child welfare journal. Politically, such as in 2018, when the Minister's Office apparently overturned DHHS's approval for my PhD data application. And personally, such as in 2020, when Gwen and her family decided I was *persona non grata* after discovering we are not genetically related. I experienced the rejection by my official maternal family as another abandonment in relation to my adoption, but also as a punishment for having exercised my adult adoptee voice.

Anyway, I took the hint. I've not initiated any communication with Gwen since receiving her 'begone' card in February 2020. Nor has Gwen initiated any contact with me. The only member of Gwen's family with whom I continued to have any contact is one of her sons, though for reasons on both sides, our text exchanges and phone conversations became less frequent and eventually stopped altogether in mid-2022.

These unhappy outcomes are unanticipated consequences of past forced mother-child separation and closed adoption practices in Victoria. Those practices enabled and concealed my misidentification as a newborn baby and led me to establish and invest in relationships with wrongly identified maternal family members. The unwanted and unbidden ending of those relationships as a result of me pursuing my true family relationships has been associated with more distress, more trauma, more losses and more grief, not only for me but for numerous other individuals as well. This is unfair on each and every one of us.

CHAPTER 3

Piecing Penny
Together Again

2019: Seeking accurate information

I was 56 by the time it was confirmed in 2019 that I was genetically unrelated to the natural mother identified in my official adoption records. It was painful to realise I had invested three decades of my life—almost all my adulthood—exploring and integrating a culture of origin that wasn't mine, and more than two decades nurturing wrongly founded maternal family relationships. I took an AncestryDNA test in 2016 seeking a missing piece of information about my paternal family—to discover who I looked like. But now there were more missing pieces of information about both my maternal and paternal families than available pieces, like an incomplete jigsaw puzzle that had accidentally been dropped, resulting in many more pieces being lost. As well as feeling sad and disappointed, I also felt unmoored, frustrated and angry, very angry.

Fuelling my anger was an overwhelming sense of injustice; of having been morally wronged; of having been duped, not once but twice, of my birthrights to my natural family relationships, culture and identity by draconian policies and practices inflicted on me as a vulnerable infant. I felt powerless and abhorred being the subject of two unlucky 'sliding door' moments that had hijacked my life and, by association, the lives of numerous other people as well. It wasn't fair. Still, I was determined to not let those feelings overwhelm me. Dealing with the impacts of forced mother-child separation and closed adoption practices had already ruled my life, but uncovering an additional layer of mistreatment through misidentification, whether accidental or intentional, didn't have to ruin it, too.

I realised that I needed to go back to the beginning and seek information about both sides of my natural family. Obviously, that meant starting with my mother: "There is a story behind every-thing. But behind all [our] stories is always [our] mother's because hers is where [ours] begins."[66] I needed to find the real facts about my conception and birth, organise them, integrate them into the apparently endless puzzle of my identity, piece myself together again, and heal. I needed to channel the Greek goddess Athena. I needed to weave in the new pieces of information, new family and cultural connections, like different-coloured threads to form a new whole me. My need to search for my natural family members was as deep and primal as it had ever been, and now it was also urgent. It wasn't a question of whether I wanted to search, rather a matter of how soon it could be done. I realised that both my parents would be elderly if they were even still alive and I couldn't bear the thought of missing the opportunity to discover who they are, reach out and potentially meet them, should they be willing.

So, in May 2019, within a week of having received Gwen's AncestryDNA test results, I lodged an application seeking my *real* adoption and related records with the Victorian Government's

---

66 Attributed to Mitch Albom, as quoted by Andi Willis in 'Inspiring Quotes About Family and Family History' (2022).

Adoption Information Service (AIS).[67] Apparently, it was the first time AIS had been approached by an adopted person who believed they were misidentified at birth. In a way it was a relief to be able to share the burden of my situation with a government authority, the very purpose of which is to assist people like me who've been separated from their natural family members through an adoption in the state of Victoria. But I also felt fragile, anxious about how I'd cope if no information about my real natural mother could be found, and strange to be on the receiving end of a service provided by my own social work profession—a field to which I had devoted a large part of my career. Still, I also fully agreed with Bruce, ever positive, who quickly pointed out that I'd "fallen with my bum in a bucket" (translation: "I was lucky") in regard to the AIS Manager, Angela Karavidas (known as 'Ange'), being someone with whom I'd previously had positive interactions when I worked with the Victorian Government's Intercountry Adoption Program, and also being someone who is Greek-Australian and speaks fluent Greek. Given my unique circumstances, Ange led the management of my case herself, working in conjunction with other AIS program staff, especially Erin Connell.

In June 2019, some five weeks after lodgement of my application, AIS organised a meeting with me in which they delivered some unexpected news. They had identified a Greek woman they strongly believed was my real natural mother! She was still alive and resided in Greece, having returned there with her husband and their children in the early 1970s. AIS had even found her current address and phone number. They also discovered that my putative mother had arrived in Melbourne from Greece by ship; that she was a single young woman, and lived in metropolitan Melbourne when I was born in March 1963; and that she gave me "a good

---

67   AIS was actually then known as FIND (Family Information Networks and Discovery).

Greek name," but not Penelope. My late adoptive parents named me Penelope, which had felt strangely more meaningful ever since Ancestry confirmed that my DNA test hadn't been mixed up in their lab. This included prompting me uncomfortably to question whether Dad and Mum did, in fact, know about my Greek heritage but chose to never disclose it to me. But I could never believe they would have pretended not to know about it, that they would have outright lied to me.

In Greek mythology, Penelope[68] is famous for her faithfulness to her husband, the Greek hero Odysseus, King of Ithaca, during his 20-year absence which began when he was called to fight in the Trojan War. During that time, Penelope devised various strategies to delay having to remarry. One of those strategies involved pretending to weave a burial shroud for Odysseus's father and promising to choose a new husband from her more than 100 suitors on its completion. But Penelope undid part of the shroud every night so that it would never be completed. Unlike the Penelope of Greek mythology, however, I've always been known by a diminutive of the name, Penny, which I've always much preferred to the formality of Penelope. More importantly, in contrast to the Penelope of Greek mythology, I did not intentionally undo any of my cloth and I was striving to finish weaving it sooner rather than later!

AIS also told me, based on her identity photo at the time of her migration to Australia in 1962, that my putative mother and I looked very much alike. I was delighted! After a lifetime of seeing no particular physical resemblance to anyone, sharing a resemblance with my mother represented a dream come true. I was impatient to see her photo. However, AIS could only provide non-identifying information and advised that I would need to apply to the County Court of Victoria for release of my mother's identifying

---

68   See the entry for 'Penelope' on Wikipedia.

information—including her precious photo. Meanwhile, AIS agreed to reach out to my mother in Greece on my behalf with a view to developing a relationship with her and requesting that she take a DNA test to confirm our genetic relationship.

By the end of the meeting my head was spinning and I felt as if I might bounce off the office walls. I recall floating along the streets of Melbourne's CBD in a haze afterwards but little of the journey home. The information about my mother was a lot to take in during a meeting I'd naively attended on my own, thinking it would involve only an update on AIS's search progress rather than disclosure of any relevant details. I hadn't expected AIS to be able to discover so much about my mother so soon.

Within two weeks of the meeting with AIS, I received notification that the examiners of my PhD thesis had recommended I be awarded the Degree of Doctor of Philosophy without further examination or amendment. I was excited, very excited, not to mention also relieved in relation to my academic achievement. But those feelings paled in comparison to my elation regarding the tantalising possibility of obtaining identifying information about and—I couldn't help but daydream—maybe even having contact with my mother. While AIS endeavoured to engage her by phone, once again I found myself metaphorically holding my breath.

My next meeting with AIS took place at the end of July 2019. This time, sensibly, I asked Bruce to accompany me for support. AIS advised us they'd used an accredited Greek interpreter, as was departmental practice, and had made three phone calls to my mother. Apparently she identified herself and confirmed my birth and relinquishment. But she then said only, "It's too late," before abruptly hanging up. AIS shared that my mother arrived in Melbourne several months before my birth, and that she married a Greek man in Melbourne later the same year she delivered me. The parents returned, with their children, in the early 1970s to Greece where they've since resided in a village where extended

43

family also live. The link with their particular region of Greece was consistent with the regional location of my genetic relatives and ancestors that was strongly indicated in my 23andMe test results.

AIS advised that they now planned to prepare a letter for translation into Greek before sending to my mother, which would provide enough information for her to make an informed decision about future contact with me. AIS recommended that I hold off applying to the County Court for my mother's identifying information until they'd done as much as possible to conclusively confirm (i.e. through DNA testing) that she is my mother. I affirmed that I would respect my mother's decision regarding future contact, including if after receiving AIS's letter she continued to express that she wanted no contact with me. Painful as that would be, I felt strongly that it was also the right thing to do.

Without disclosing any identifying details, AIS also informed us they'd identified an adopted woman whose identity they believed mine was swapped with after birth—that is, Gwen's real eldest daughter. AIS then asked after Gwen. I explained that our relationship had become strained, that I was unsure whether she had ever sought or received any adoption-specific support and, in any event, that I thought it unlikely she was receiving any such support now. AIS indicated they would contact Gwen directly to ascertain how she was faring and to offer her support and assistance in relation to the adoption of her daughter. I was pleased for Gwen, irrespective of the state of our relationship. Gwen was forcibly separated from her first baby for the purpose of adoption and deserved such support.

Meanwhile, there was a frustrating delay in AIS getting their letter translated into Greek and sent to my mother. The delay was due to bureaucratic reasons associated with the unexpected and untimely machinery of government transfer of Victoria's Adoption Services from the Department of Health and Human Services (DHHS) to the Department of Justice and Community Safety

(DJCS) at the beginning of July 2019. The rationale for the transfer remains unclear as it was never publicised, which is strange given that Adoption Services is not a natural fit for the government department that also runs policing, courts and prisons. For example, the transfer was not recommended by the Victorian Law Reform Commission (VLRC) in its wide-ranging review of the *Adoption Act 1984* completed in 2017.[69]

In August 2019, I commenced my first term of a beginner's Greek language course. I figured this was something constructive I could do to increase my knowledge of Greek culture as well as my communication skills for when I visited Greece—which I fully intended to do with Bruce and Patrick as soon as practicable, even if I was unable to meet any family members there.

Later the same month I also attended a conference, 'DNA Down Under', which focused on using DNA to assist in searching for family history.[70] At the conference I met Brad Argent, Senior Director, International Programming, with Ancestry.[71] I disclosed to him the discovery of my Greek ethnicity through an AncestryDNA test in 2016 and how it had led to the further discovery that I was misidentified prior to my adoption. Brad was intrigued with my story and gave me contact details for Claire Forster of Artemis Films which produces *Every Family Has A Secret* (EFHAS) for SBS.[72] Brad said he'd never done this before and explained that EFHAS would be able to utilise AncestryDNA resources to assist me in finding, learning about, and hopefully also connecting with my natural relatives. I told Brad that I was nowhere near ready for my story to be made public, nevertheless he encouraged me to contact Claire if and when I was ever ready.

---

69 See the VLRC's *Review of the Adoption Act 1984: Report* (2017). Op. cit.
70 See DNA Down Under (23 August 2019) 'Melbourne'.
71 See Bryony (2 June 2016) 'The DNA Journey: Powered by AncestryDNA'.
72 See Artemis Media (2022) *Every Family Has A Secret*; and SBS (2022) SBS On Demand's *Every Family Has A Secret* and *Who Are We?*

I realised that involvement with EFHAS was another option should AIS be unsuccessful in progressing their engagement with my mother in Greece.

I contacted AIS at the beginning of October 2019 to check where things were at with their letter to my mother. They expected it to be sent with tracking within the next fortnight. They also planned to follow up with a phone call and had decided that Ange should speak directly in Greek, rather than through an interpreter. They thought the alternative, less formal, approach may be more effective in establishing rapport with my mother. AIS reported there had been other discussions in relation to my case and it was subsequently agreed that there was no reason to withhold my original first name, though this did not apply to my original family name because that could identify my mother. Ange explained that my original first name was a gift from my mother in a Greek tradition of naming the first daughter after the maternal grandmother. (To my ears, my Greek first name sounds beautiful and also has a beautiful meaning in Greek.) I'd learned enough basic Greek language by that time to be able to handwrite my Greek name in Greek, which I promptly did with a big black Texta on a yellow sticky label and displayed it prominently on the fridge in our open plan kitchen for months afterward. Learning my Greek first name made me feel special. It made me feel that my mother did love me as a baby, even if she apparently refused to allow herself to love me now as an adult.

By late November 2019, I was anxious waiting for AIS's letter to get to Greece and for a response, any response at all, from my mother. So I arranged for Bruce and me to again meet with AIS, this time to discuss my planned application for release of identifying information about my mother and to clarify exactly what I needed to request of the County Court of Victoria. A few days later, at the beginning of December 2019, I submitted my Application for Release of Information under section 99(1) or section 100(1) of the *Adoption Act 1984* to the County Court for all relevant records and information pertaining to the correct identity of my natural mother, thus also pertaining to my correct original identity. I waited anxiously once again for an outcome that was beyond my control. AIS indicated that such applications were generally resolved within four weeks, perhaps up to six weeks on this occasion, given the Christmas break was approaching. Of course, the wait would feel interminable and frustrating irrespective of how long or short the actual time period involved. Indeed, I already lacked patience and was struggling to maintain focus on my Greek language lessons, so decided not to re-enrol for the New Year.

At least in the meantime I could look forward to my PhD conferral, having booked into a ceremony scheduled for late afternoon on 17 December. It turned out to be a very hot and very humid summer's day in Melbourne, uncomfortable for all in attendance at the historic Royal Exhibition Buildings, which have neither air conditioning nor fans. It was even steamier for those of us wearing the extra layers of academic regalia. In my case, this was a black broad-brimmed velvet hat with red tassels and a black long-sleeved robe with red satin trim. But as it turned out, the seasonally-inappropriate garb was not the biggest challenge of the ceremony for me. For starters, more than five hundred University of Melbourne graduands were having their degrees conferred, despite the ceremony being restricted to the Faculty of Medicine, Dentistry and Health Sciences, and the PhD graduands would be last to receive theirs. Nevertheless, in a wonderful feat of organisation, in alphabetical order for each type of Masters degree, each graduand in their rightful turn ascended the front stairs to the stage, had their name announced as they received their degree from a Faculty Dean, and then posed for a photo with said Dean before exiting down the same stairs by which they'd arrived.

Proud of having persevered to complete my studies, I waited uncharacteristically patiently for the PhD conferrals. I was basking in the knowledge that I thoroughly deserved the piece of paper I was about to receive, and thoroughly enjoyed the anticipation and excitement as my turn approached in the middle of the almost 30-strong PhD group. We were treated to considerably more pomp and ceremony than the hoi polloi. In alphabetical turn, not only was our name announced with our new title, "Dr ...," but we accessed the stage from the side and waited at a mark onstage while a blurb summarising our research was read out. Only then did the Dean signal the graduand to step forward, shake hands and pose for a photo with him/her holding their degree face out to display the graduand's full name and degree details.

Unfortunately, my turn went slightly less smoothly than it did for the other PhD graduands. First, the Academic Board Member introducing me stumbled slightly in pronouncing my name. I wondered how hard it could be to pronounce 'Penelope Kathleen Mackieson' compared with the much trickier Asian, Indian, European and South American names that seemed to have been correctly pronounced throughout the long ceremony up to that very moment—*my* moment. Then the Academic Board Member also stumbled slightly in reading out my research blurb, nothing major but not cleanly delivered. Next, even dodgier, the Dean held me for so long on the mark that I made a few hesitant steps too soon in his direction and, embarrassed, had to retrace them. When the Dean finally signalled me to proceed, he shook my hand, said the obligatory "Congratulations," then discreetly added that the administrative staff couldn't find my degree at that moment but, not to worry, someone would find me after the official ceremony and give it to me then. Seriously? I'd worked hard for three-and-a-half years for this moment, this big moment. It was dreadfully anti-climactic, a total fizzer. The official film of my conferral captures the strangeness of it all, though somehow I managed to keep most of the confusion from my face and maintain a calm expression. Likewise, my formal photo with the Dean shows me smiling remarkably genuinely under the circumstances and shaking his hand while, with the other, he held a plain cardboard folder bearing the university logo instead of my doctoral degree. I felt duped again.

Even while it was happening, all I could think was how fitting. It's not just a feeling, I really am an imposter in my own life. Of the hundreds of graduands awarded their degrees in the ceremony in which I was awarded mine, there was only one mix-up with the paperwork and, of course, it had to be with mine. I realised that the university would have had no idea, and would probably have been mortified if it had known, about the awful coincidence for me in addition to my big moment having been spoiled. I could only shake my head and wonder how many more ridiculous mix-ups could happen to me in my lifetime. How many more times would I be subjected to some mishap or incompetence—or malfeasance?— at the hands of officials? And how much more could I tolerate before becoming paranoid about a conspiracy to undermine my mental health and well-being?

In fairness to the university, soon after the ceremony ended an administrator did quickly locate me, apologise and hand over my actual paper degree. This happened before I even managed to find my family and friends in the buzzing flush-faced crowd. I took my degree directly to the framing stall, then left the framed product with my guests. I briefly shared with them what had happened before I took off to return my hired academic regalia. Unbeknown to me until later when celebrating over dinner at a nearby restaurant, my degree was originally inserted into its frame upside down. The problem was unobtrusive but a keen-eyed friend, Keri Whitehead, noticed a gold university logo printed on the matboard inside the frame the wrong way up. Bruce dashed to the framing stall to have it fixed before I re-joined my guests. He knew full well that if I'd been the one to spot the issue it may have triggered pent up tears of rage and a swearing tirade for the ages.

2020: Accessing identifying information

Four weeks elapsed from the date I lodged my County Court application, Christmas 2019 came and went, then six weeks elapsed, seven weeks ... Meanwhile I maintained close contact with AIS who informed me late in January 2020 that their report, part of the process involved in my County Court application, had been hand delivered to the court. The following month I contacted the court to check on the status of my application and, by the beginning of March, was anxious that its resolution might be further delayed due to administrative impacts from the COVID-19 pandemic. I'd made bookings for our first ever trip to Greece for September-October 2020, including flights and a chartered yacht cruise around the Small Cyclades in the Aegean Sea, all of which was suddenly at risk of cancellation for the same reason. The pandemic was looming as another hurdle in my quest for information about my identity and direct experience of my culture of origin. My frustration quickly compounded when my workplace cautiously instructed office-based staff to commence working from home even before the Victorian Government decreed its first official lockdown. I was not happy about any of it.

Throughout March I was progressively forced to cancel the bookings for our trip to Greece. The state's first official lockdown commenced on 31 March and, by the end of the third week, I was ropable. For the first time in my life I detested living in Victoria. If I'd wanted to live in a country under a draconian regime, I would have moved to China before this. I felt trapped, helpless, hostage to sweeping policies ostensibly aiming for zero COVID-19 infections that seemed doomed to fail from the outset because of excessive fearmongering[73] and poor targeting and implementation to protect

---

73 Carmen Lawrence discusses the effective use of fear in politics in her aptly named book, *Fear and Politics* (2006), Op. cit. The book focuses heavily on John Howard's Prime Ministership of Australia from 1996 to 2007. But in my view, much of what

the most vulnerable members of the community. If I'd been able to concoct an officially acceptable reason to leave Victoria and escape south to Tasmania I would have done so, irrespective of whether Bruce and Patrick could accompany me. They also sensed that the stage was set for a long pandemic for Melbournians in general and our household in particular. Unfortunately, we were correct.

Late in March 2020, AIS informed me of the results of forensic DNA tests taken by Gwen and the adopted woman whose identity they believed mine had been swapped with. Both parties had consented to me being told. The DNA testing confirmed that their genetic relationship is mother-daughter, and AIS had already advised the County Court of this. I subsequently received a letter from the court on 6 April advising it had "communicated" with my "potential birth mother" and the person I was "potentially switched with at birth" seeking their consent by 30 June 2020 to the release of identifying information. The letter advised I would be contacted after that date if any objections were received. I was annoyed. I felt like others had been given the opportunity to deny me access to information about my identity. I felt like their wishes would be prioritised ahead of my needs, my human rights. Meanwhile, it had already been four months since I lodged my application with the County Court and the end of June seemed light years away. Yet more anxious waiting for an outcome beyond my control. I wasn't getting any better at waiting.

In the interim, AIS contacted me in June 2020 and informed me of a phone conversation they'd had earlier that day with my putative mother in Greece—Ange had spoken directly in Greek without an interpreter, as they'd previously decided. The reason AIS called her is that they were concerned the County Court had sent her a letter without them having first been able to fully

---

Lawrence wrote could also have been the playbook for Daniel Andrews' Premiership of Victoria during the COVID-19 pandemic.

explain to her what the letter was about. My mother acknowledged to Ange that she'd received the letter from the County Court, but made it clear she had no intention of responding to it. The phone conversation apparently went for some time, during which Ange was able to develop some connection with my mother, only ending when my mother indicated that one of her sons had arrived. My mother explained to Ange that her husband had passed away, that her sons don't know she had a child who was adopted, and that she had never told anyone else about her adopted baby. However, she apparently yelled this so loudly down the phone that AIS figured the whole neighbourhood probably knew now.

Meanwhile, Ange was able to explain to my mother that her baby, now known as Penny, was trying to obtain identifying information about her, that this was because I recently discovered through DNA testing that the mother I was officially led to believe decades ago was mine was not actually my mother. My mother responded, "Well, that's your fault!" Ange explained to my mother that I was misidentified while at the Queen Victoria Memorial Hospital (QVMH). Ange also explained that the adopted woman whose identity AIS believed mine had been swapped with was confirmed through DNA testing as the daughter of the woman identified as my mother in my adoption records.

My mother reportedly said all she needed to know was that I'd been given to "a good family." My mother told Ange that she was young and very innocent when she conceived me. She said, as a single young woman newly arrived in a foreign country without being able to speak English, she realised she wouldn't be able to care for her baby. So the hospital offered her adoption, assuring her that her baby "would be given to a good family." Ange confirmed this, adding that I was well cared for and well-educated.

Ange also explained to my mother that I had a right to know my original family and cultural heritage, that I planned to visit the place in Greece where my family came from, and that my brothers have a right to know they have an older sister. My mother reiterated that she didn't want me to contact her and that "it is too late" for us to meet. Ange responded that I was equally assertive in seeking her identifying details. It seemed that my mother and I may have similarly determined personalities.

Eventually, in July 2020, more than seven months after I'd lodged my application, Her Honour Judge Sandra Davis of the County Court of Victoria ordered that the Secretary, DJCS, release to me information relating to Donna,[74] the adopted woman whose identity mine had been swapped with. Her Honour made the order in chambers without a hearing, despite my request for one, and without any direct communication with me. I was immensely relieved but also annoyed. Sure, I'd finally obtained the Court's approval to access identifying information about my putative Greek mother. But the process was protracted and infantilising, and I was unclear whether either of those things were unanticipated impacts of the COVID-19 pandemic or business as usual for complex post-adoption matters. Whatever. It was time to focus on the release of the records. To that end, within a week of the County Court order having been made I met with AIS to clarify the documents involved and the process for their release to me.

By far the most exciting part of the meeting was when AIS verbally relayed the key identifying facts about my mother and me so I wouldn't have to wait until I received the documents. It was a veritable smorgasbord of information, including my mother's first name, Georgia;[75] her maiden family name, Zagarelou; her date of birth; the name of the place she originally came from in Greece; and the *pièce de resistance*, the full name she gave me when she registered my birth. It was better than winning Tattslotto! At last I knew my mother's identity and a significant portion of my own

---

74 "Donna" is an alias first name.
75 "Georgia" is an alias first name.

original identity. The information provided to me also included the name of the ship on which my mother travelled from Greece; the date she arrived in Melbourne; her husband's name, the date of their marriage, and the name and address of the church in which they were married in Melbourne; and the names of the province, town and village in Greece where she now lived. Bruce and I were set to do some serious Google-snooping before I even received the documents containing scanned copies of the relevant records.

During the meeting with AIS, we also discussed possible next steps to correct my birth records in the context of the limitations of the relevant Births, Deaths and Marriages (BDM) legislation and procedures. The primary options presented by AIS both involved a second application to the County Court. The application would request either: (a) that BDM change my original birth registration under section 42 or 43 of the *Births, Deaths and Marriages Registration Act 1996* by removing Gwen's details from my original birth certificate; or (b) discharge of my adoption under section 19 of the *Adoption Act 1984* on the grounds that my adoption was done improperly/unlawfully because of my misidentification, which would enable reinstatement of my original birth registration as the baby born to Georgia. AIS believed that option (a) could also result in the Court choosing to change Donna's original birth registration by removing Georgia's details and replacing them with Gwen's, because it already had the DNA evidence supporting Gwen and Donna's mother-daughter relationship. However, without DNA evidence confirming my mother-daughter relationship with Georgia, even if Gwen's details were removed from my original birth registration, the Court could choose not to replace those details with Georgia's. This would leave blank entries for both my mother and my father on my original birth certificate because the Court may consider both their identities, not only my father's, to be unverified. To me, option (a) sounded half-arsed and totally unfair—Donna could end up with her records being fixed but not me, yet I was the one seeking for mine to be fixed. But in regard to option (b), I'd never before had a reason to consider seeking discharge of my adoption. It was doing my head in.

AIS asked me specifically what I was inclined to do. I replied that whatever else I did later on, in the meantime I would seek removal of Gwen's details from my original birth certificate as quickly as possible because it is a fact that she is not my natural mother. I explained my motivation to pursue the matter, that it was to integrate the facts of my identity; that I was not seeking to deny my adoption; that what I really wanted was not available in Victoria, being an integrated birth certificate that truthfully and accurately records the details of my natural parents and my adoptive parents. I didn't think I wanted to discharge my adoption and change my legal name because it was the name I'd been known by all my life from three weeks of age. But who would I be if I ended up with an 'original' birth certificate that recorded both my natural parents as unknown? I was suddenly overwhelmed and teary about the possibility of my identity becoming even more unanchored should AIS be unable to persuade Georgia to take a DNA test to confirm our relationship.

We discussed my QVMH medical records, too. It was only then that I understood AIS had not specifically requested any QVMH medical records from Monash Health in the course of their investigation in relation to my identity (and Donna's). The AIS explained that they had searched archives held by the Victorian Government and discovered a QVMH register containing consecutive entries for Georgia and Gwen, which identified their babies for adoption—this clue led AIS to ultimately confirm that Donna's identity was the one with which mine had been swapped.

When the records ordered for release arrived two days later, I made a beeline for the photo of Georgia taken in 1962. I studied the photo intently, staring at it until my eyes stung. Georgia certainly looked like a young ethnically-Greek woman, but I failed to see the strong resemblance between Georgia's face and mine about which AIS staff were so confident. Sure, we both had dark hair and dark eyes but Georgia's looked black where mine were brown, and our hairlines both featured a 'widow's peak' but mine was more pointed and more sharply defined than Georgia's. Indeed, it was the differences, not the similarities, which stood out to me most. My face was more heart-shaped while Georgia's was squarer with a more defined jawline; Georgia's eyebrows and lips were fuller and her nose much neater than mine; my forehead was longer than Georgia's … Why did discerning a physical likeness to my mother have to be so damned difficult?! Was I being too picky? How ironic it would be if I actually looked more like my father and his relatives … again. Why wouldn't Georgia just do a DNA test, even if we never had any direct contact, so I could be confident she really was my mother?

I also closely examined the court records released to me. They confirmed, as relayed previously by AIS, that Donna's adoption was privately arranged by a social worker at the QVMH, apparently in liaison with "a Social Worker for the Greek Community connected with the Greek Orthodox Church in Melbourne." The thing that struck me most from the court records was the plethora of dates on which events took place in relation to Donna, different dates (aside from our shared birthday) to those relating to my adoptive placement, birth registration and finalised adoption. I decided the best way to get my head around it all and try to discern when our identities might have been switched was to collate the dates and events relating each to Donna and me in a table or spreadsheet, so I could visualise it chronologically.

On collating the table, I made an unexpected discovery. Donna, misidentified as the baby born to Georgia Zagarelou, left the QVMH six days before me. She was placed with her adoptive parents directly by a QVMH social worker on 26 March 1963, aged 16 days. However, Georgia's written consent for the adoption was 'obtained' the next day, on 27 March 1963, witnessed by a solicitor at a firm in Lonsdale Street, Melbourne, and the social worker (and Greek-English interpreter) connected with the Greek Orthodox Church. I understood that obtaining a mother's consent for the adoption of her child *after* placement of the child with the adoptive parents was unethical. But I also thought it was illegal under the *Adoption of Children Act 1958* that was in place in Victoria at the time. It was only after scrutinising the 1958 Act more recently that I realised there was no reference at all to the timing of the mother's consent being obtained, which left it wide open for exploitation and dodgy practices. Indeed, it appears some changes were made to prevent such situations in the next primary set of adoption laws in Victoria, the *Adoption of Children Act 1964*, passed the year after Donna's and my birth. In particular, section 28(1) of that Act states that

> [T]he Court shall not make an adoption order in reliance on a consent given or purporting to have been given by a person (other than the child) if it appears to the Court that—… *(b)* the consent was obtained by fraud or duress.

No doubt Georgia would have felt enormous pressure to proceed with formally consenting to the adoption of her baby given the baby (albeit misidentified) had already been given into the care of Donna's adoptive parents. In other words, it was clear to me that the adoption of Georgia's baby occurred in coercive circumstances even without having access to the relevant QVMH medical records.

A few weeks later, in August 2020, Ange informed me of a phone call she'd made the previous day to Georgia in Greece to explain the outcome of my County Court application. The conversation was reportedly brief, lasting only four or five minutes, because Georgia strongly expressed she did not wish to discuss anything to do with her past or her decision regarding the adoption of her daughter in Melbourne; that she did not want AIS to contact her ever again; and that she would not accept any contact from me, including letters. There was nothing equivocal about the meaning of Georgia's message—she wanted nothing whatsoever to do with me. Now to my Greek mother, as well as to my official but incorrect mother, I was *persona non grata*. It was not unexpected given the gist of Georgia's communications in AIS's previous phone calls to her, but it still hurt deeply to be rejected again. Another thing in my life that was unfair because of adoption.

Notwithstanding, Ange was able to both impart and obtain some important information which she rightly believed I'd want to know. Georgia was apparently emphatic that her husband was not my father, and that my father did not know of her pregnancy with me. Georgia confirmed that my father was from Greece and that he was her friend, but she refused to provide any further information about his identity or whether he was still alive. Ange said she was able to explain to Georgia that I now had access to identifying information about her, and that I was seeking rightful amendment to my original birth certificate to record her as my mother. Georgia responded that the need for this amendment was not her fault, nor anything in which she was interested. Georgia asked if I was seeking any inheritance, property or money, to which Ange replied that I was financially stable and not seeking to gain financially. Georgia reiterated her view that her daughter in Australia had no right to contact her sons in Greece and that they were not my relatives. Ange explained that I could engage with her sons (my brothers) if I chose to, that this was part of my search for my identity, and that there were no laws in Australia or Greece that prevented me from contacting them.

I subsequently called an urgent (remote) meeting with AIS, which Bruce was able to join for the first ten or so minutes. During the meeting, AIS further informed me that the DJCS had decided AIS would engage in no further outreach efforts to Georgia, given her consistent message that she wanted no further contact from either AIS or me. Other decisions made about my case were also communicated during the meeting: that AIS would not seek relevant QVMH medical records from Monash Health on my behalf, given these were not required for me to have Georgia's identifying information; that AIS would close my case now that Donna's adoption records containing Georgia's identifying information had been released to me; and that AIS would continue to pursue legal advice, which had been delayed due to the COVID-19 crisis, in regard to correcting my birth records and would advise me as soon as this was received. Despite their imminent closure of my case, AIS was obliged to correct both my records and Donna's because they knew those records were incorrect.

I was taken aback. I hadn't seen the closure of my AIS case coming. It didn't seem like a decision that Ange would have recommended or supported. It was most disappointing, especially on top of Georgia's explicit rejection of me. I indicated to AIS my reluctance to contact my brothers directly for fear of further rejection, and because I didn't want to be the person to disclose to them that they had an older sister if our mother had not already told them. I also explained that my reluctance was partly based on my concern about the small chance, in the absence of forensic DNA test results confirming our relationship, that Georgia was not in fact my mother. Indeed, I had communicated to AIS numerous times from the very beginning in May 2019 that I didn't wish to risk another wrongful reunion. Relatedly, given I was not as convinced as AIS that I shared a close facial resemblance with Georgia, if now I was expected to undertake my own outreach to my brothers in Greece, I needed more specific non-identifying information about how AIS had concluded with such confidence that Georgia was my mother. In response, AIS would only disclose that they had eliminated the other Greek mothers who gave birth at the QVMH around the time of my birth "for various reasons." AIS further maintained that providing me with the information I sought was beyond its powers under the *Adoption Act 1984* and would require me to make a further application to the County Court. This seemed to me to be preposterous, excessive, and wasteful of precious judicial resources.

I was well aware that AIS did not generally provide intermediary services to those separated by adoption. I was also well aware, due to the special circumstances of my case, that AIS had up till now been willing to provide me with as much assistance and support as I required, including outreach on my behalf, within the limits of its role. So I couldn't understand the sudden withdrawal of that assistance and support. It simply didn't make sense to me. It wasn't in keeping with the nature of our engagement, especially at such a vulnerable time when I was still digesting the identifying information about Georgia that was recently provided to me. I suspected there were other influences at play and wondered how high up in the bureaucracy the decisions about my case had been made—the Minister's Office? I realised that paranoid thinking was unhelpful, but I wasn't prepared to simply lie down and accept the DJCS's apparent abandonment of me without some pushback. I believed strongly that I needed AIS's continuing assistance— especially Ange's—to have any chance of positively connecting with my family members in Greece. At the very least I deserved a full explanation.

So, late in August 2020, I wrote to the Attorney-General (A-G), the Victorian Government Minister responsible for Adoption Services, seeking clarification regarding the scope of AIS's responsibilities in relation to helping remediate my situation. It was a calculated risk intended to leapfrog any senior bureaucratic roadblocks to the extension of AIS's assistance to me. I hoped there would be no backlash, especially for AIS because that would have been most undeserved. I began my four-and-a-half page letter to the A-G by genuinely commending the AIS staff involved with my unusual and complex case and expressing my appreciation of their responsiveness, supportiveness and professionalism. Notwithstanding, I indicated that I disagreed with the positions recently communicated to me by AIS: that QVMH medical records did not form part of the information relevant to my adoption information application; that AIS was not permitted to provide me with non-identifying information about any other Greek women who delivered babies at the QVMH around the time I was born and could potentially have given birth to me; and that it was appropriate for AIS to close my case now, before they'd pursed DNA testing with my brothers in Greece that would confirm Georgia is my mother.

I highlighted that without AIS's continued assistance I was stuck. The reasons being that I had no access to official identifying information about my two putative brothers, who AIS told me were born here in Melbourne; that without my own original birth record corrected to reflect that I'm Georgia's daughter I was unable to verify for BDM purposes my eligibility to obtain identifying information about my brothers; and that even the County Court order made in July 2020 failed to explicitly conclude that I'm Georgia's daughter. While Her Honour Judge Davis was apparently "satisfied that circumstances exist which make it desirable that the order be made," she did not specify those circumstances in the order.

I argued that if AIS was to now close my case, as had apparently been decided, leaving me to undertake my own outreach with my putative maternal family members, I needed to be confident of the process by which AIS had identified them. I argued that this was entirely reasonable given the outrageous inaccuracy of the identifying information recorded in the first set of adoption records released to me by AIS in 1990. I also argued that without further assistance from AIS I was effectively in no better position than when I first lodged my application with them in May 2019. AIS had quickly identified Georgia as my natural mother, but from information I was not permitted to access and which AIS claimed it was unable to elaborate for me. Meanwhile, AIS had not yet verified the accuracy of its belief regarding the identity of my mother through DNA testing. Therefore, from my perspective, AIS had not completed its task; still had a duty of care toward me; and was responsible for following through on verifying the identity of my mother, as far as reasonably possible. Finally, as I had relied on AIS's advice and had always fully complied with the processes it recommended to me, I asserted that termination of AIS's support would represent yet another abandonment in my lived experience of adoption, which I did not deserve. I deliberately laid it on even more thickly by describing the planned closure of my case as further institutional neglect in relation to my forced and closed adoption, especially when the legal validity of my adoption was still unclear.

I was frustrated and angry but hoped I'd managed to control it enough for my letter to the A-G to sound reasonable and draw a constructive response. Within a few days of sending it, I had my first session with a private counsellor in relation to my situation. I'd been thinking about seeking counselling for some time and was encouraged to follow up after a discussion with a good friend in the adoption community, as I knew it was unfair to be constantly offloading onto my nearest and dearest. Even though it was pre-arranged, the timing of that first counselling session couldn't have been better. I had a further six sessions with the counsellor over the next ten months.

AIS contacted me early in September 2020 to let me know they'd received my letter to the A-G from senior management and that a formal response to my questions would be provided in a Ministerial reply in due course. AIS expressed that we seemed to have had a miscommunication in regard to the closure of my case. I maintained a different view, which was shared by Bruce who attended the first part of the meeting when AIS advised me of the

DJCS's decisions. Regardless, I was both pleased and relieved on being informed that my case remained open with AIS; that AIS was most willing to reach out to my brothers in Greece and would now proceed to contact Yiannis,[76] one of Georgia's sons; and that the legal advice AIS was seeking about how to correct my records would likely now be expedited to inform the impending Ministerial response to my letter to the A-G.

The next month, October 2020, AIS updated me on their outreaches to my brothers in Greece. Disappointingly, they were yet to receive any response. AIS also informed me that no other female babies were born to Greek mothers at the QVMH on or around the date of my birth, making me wonder how that information could ever have been considered identifying; hence AIS's confidence that they had accurately identified Georgia as my real natural mother. Indeed, I felt considerably more assured of my daughter relationship to Georgia from that point onward. Notwithstanding, there was still no proof. Despite AIS's numerous efforts, progress in relation to connecting with my brothers and obtaining DNA evidence seemed to have hit a brick wall. It seemed an appropriate time to initiate 'plan B'.

So, a few days later I phoned Claire Forster, the producer of EFHAS. Claire confirmed that Brad Argent from Ancestry had never previously given a potential participant in the show her direct contact details. As Brad had anticipated, Claire was very interested in my story and felt EFHAS could tell it. Claire asked me to consider sharing my DNA data with EFHAS's genetic genealogist to pursue DNA matches and compile a family tree, to which I consented. Notwithstanding, Claire cautioned that taking DNA tests is not popular among Greek (and Italian) people and therefore it may be difficult to find reasonably close matches for

---

76 "Yiannis" is an alias first name.

me. Indeed, nothing much seemed to happen in relation to my engagement with EFHAS until the New Year.

In January 2021, Claire informed me that EFHAS's genetic genealogist was having difficulty developing my family tree because my DNA matches with relatives were too distant, just as she'd forewarned. However, a telehealth session with a psychologist was organised for me in March 2021 as part of the assessment process for my participation in EFHAS. A few days later, in a window between the third and fourth COVID-19 lockdowns in Victoria, I was flown to Adelaide to film the introduction of my story. At least it felt like something was progressing in relation to EFHAS's efforts to connect with my extended family. However, it was evident they were continuing to struggle when they contacted me in November 2021 to request my permission to upload my DNA data to the GEDmatch, FamilyTreeDNA and MyHeritage databases. Of course, I agreed. I had nothing to lose and it meant further seeds would be planted that might germinate and bear fruit at some unknown time in the future.

Meanwhile, in November 2020, AIS told me they'd written to Monash Health requesting QVMH records for me and my mother but no such records were found. So AIS then requested more details about what happened to the QVMH records for Gwen/Donna and Georgia/me. Monash Health's FOI Unit replied in December 2020, and AIS forwarded me the reply to avoid the wasted paperwork and time they anticipated would otherwise be involved in my inevitable request for it under FOI provisions. I didn't interpret this in a critical way because it was clear AIS understood my determination to find out what really happened to my hospital records. In their reply to AIS, Monash Health advised that they'd conducted "a thorough and diligent search" through which they located a patient listing for Georgia, although the listing misspelled both her first and last names. Monash Health also identified a hospital number for Georgia's QVMH patient records, but no physical records associated with that number could be found. Further, they could not find any patient listing or medical records for Georgia's baby, or for Gwen or Gwen's baby.

Monash Health also stated, just as they'd indicated to me several times previously, that the QVMH relocated to Monash Medical Centre in Clayton in 1987 and that "a destruction of medical records was undertaken in accordance [with] the Disposal Schedule at the time." My view of the validity of Monash Health's apparent disposal of my mother's and my medical records in 1987 was quite different, given that the *Adoption Act 1984* (the principal adoption legislation in effect at the time and since) specifically prohibits the destruction, removal or concealment of records in respect of adoptions.[77] While the Act does not define 'adoption records' or 'adoption information', it clearly suggests a more encompassing interpretation than one restricted to the adoption documents lodged with and issued by the Court. Furthermore, I understood that the QVMH was an approved private adoption agency. As I was identified for adoption from birth (probably prior to my birth), it is reasonable to expect that the QVMH would have implemented a more, rather than less, encompassing interpretation of the adoption information and records it held in relation to me and my mother.

Regardless, Monash Health was unable "to locate any lists of the destroyed records" that would confirm the patient records pertaining to Georgia/me and Gwen/Donna had, in fact, been destroyed. I appreciated AIS's follow up with Monash Health in regard to my QVMH records, even if I'd had to push for it through the A-G, and even though the outcome was curiously inconclusive. Indeed, I remained frustrated, unsatisfied and unable to dismiss the matter of my QVMH records. The QVMH's mistreatment

---

77 Section 85 of the *Adoption Act 1984* (Vic) outlines the relevant provisions in relation to preserving records in respect of adoptions.

and misidentification of those records was emblematic of its mistreatment and misidentification of *me* as a newborn baby.

I had another discussion with AIS in November 2020, too, this one in relation to BDM's limited capacity to correct my original birth record. BDM had confirmed they were able to remove Gwen's details from my original birth record but were unable to amend my official 'original' name, which would have to remain the name that Gwen gave her baby—unless I made another application to the County Court. It was clear, therefore, that even if the option of an integrated birth certificate was available in Victoria, mine would record incorrect details about my birth and original identity. It remained unclear, however, whether my adoption was legally valid given my misidentification at the time my Adoption Order was granted. I figured if my Adoption Order was not legally valid that I may need to make a different application to the County Court or, perhaps, may not even need to make another application to the County Court at all. So, I renewed my request for advice in writing from DJCS specifically in relation to the legal status of my adoption.

The following month, AIS contacted me to provide an update in relation to a phone conversation they'd just had with Georgia. The conversation had occurred inadvertently when they were attempting to contact Georgia's other son, Nikos.[78] Georgia unexpectedly opened up to Ange and they ended up speaking for over half an hour. Georgia confided that she didn't know she was pregnant when she left Greece for Australia in 1962 with the intention of marrying her husband—which she did the following year, several months after my birth. Georgia reiterated that she never told her husband about her first baby and that the baby's father also did not know, though she persisted with her refusal to confirm whether my father was still alive. She said it remained

78 "Nikos" is an alias first name.

"a dark shame," that she had carried the secret her whole life, and that her baby having been taken away was "a haunting memory" for her—a wound which had been re-opened through Ange's contact. Georgia shared that she'd felt alone and isolated, that she didn't see any other options at the time, and that the Greek social worker told her she had no choice but to relinquish her baby for adoption. Even according to her own words, then, Georgia had been coerced into relinquishing her baby for adoption, consistent with what I'd learned from Donna's court records.

Georgia told Ange that she held her baby for a short while after the birth, that she cried a lot and didn't understand what was happening. My heart broke for Georgia who was obviously traumatised by her experience. Ange was able to explain the AIS program to Georgia and that I'd been searching for her for a long time. Nevertheless, Georgia pleaded with Ange to stop pursuing the matter with her and her other children. Georgia said she "would die" before she would do a DNA test to confirm our relationship, again saying "it's too late." I empathised with Georgia's pain in relation to the opening of her deep wound concerning the circumstances of my conception, birth and relinquishment. Yet Georgia's response deeply wounded me, too. From my perspective it would never be too late for us to meet and heal at least some of our wounds while Georgia was alive. It was hard for me to understand why Georgia couldn't see that, too. Why did Georgia's past shame have to rule her current response? Shame from ex-nuptial pregnancy was a social construct that Georgia applied to herself then. But she could choose to not apply it now, not accept it. After all, in Australia, the latest census statistics show that almost 40% of babies are born to parents not in a registered marriage[79] and, in Victoria, becoming a single parent is not only accepted but actually facilitated by the Government through the provision

---

79 See Australian Bureau of Statistics (2021) 'Births, Australia'.

of public fertility care services.[80] Of course, I appreciate that Western adoption is deeply grounded in shame. But while Georgia perpetuates her shame, she perpetuates mine as well. Shame on those of us born 'illegitimate', born 'bastard'. Shame on those of us who shouldn't have been born at all! Shame on *me*!

2021: Reclaiming and integrating my identity

Eventually, in February 2021, I received a sensitively-worded detailed letter from Victoria's new A-G in response to my letter of August 2020 to her predecessor. The letter summarised information I'd already received directly from AIS. It also explained that

> [A]doption information provided to applicants includes information from the records of the agency who arranged the adoption as well as information provided to the Court when the adoption order was made … The [Adoption] Act defines adoption information more broadly than information from the records of the agency and the Court. Adoption information may include information sought from hospitals, Births, Deaths and Marriages, and wardship records held by the Department of Health. The Act, however, is silent in relation to the scope of information that can be provided and when and how it can be shared (and with whom).

The letter did not include any specific legal advice regarding the status of my adoption, or the administrative or legal process(es) required to correct my original birth record. However, it confirmed that AIS and BDM were "now working together to progress the questions" I had raised, and that BDM was seeking legal advice on the BDM Registrar's powers under the Act "to amend entries to the Register that were ordered by the County Court."

In April 2021, Nora O'Connor, the new BDM Registrar, contacted me to confirm BDM would do all it could within the

---

80   See Department of Health (2022) 'Public Fertility Care Services'.

relevant legislation to assist me, and a meeting was arranged for us to discuss the complexities of my situation. Indeed, those complexities had become all-consuming, dominating my waking thoughts to the extent that I was no longer able to focus properly on my work. Although I had previously sought and received approval to reduce the number of my working days per week, I remained so preoccupied that I decided it was best to resign from my job, and I finished up at the end of April. I didn't have the capacity to fight against the derailment of my career at the same time I was fighting against the derailment of my identity.

The following month I received a letter from Nora confirming the content of the discussion during our meeting. This included that BDM only had the power to remove Gwen's name from my pre-adoptive birth record and that it would need to apply to the County Court to correct my original pre-adoptive name—just as AIS had previously advised I would need to do in November 2020. I confirmed that I wished to proceed with the correction outlined and, on 1 June, BDM advised they had "now corrected" my pre-adoptive birth certificate leaving the 'Mother' field blank. BDM agreed to Express Post the corrected document to me but, ten days later, it had not yet arrived. So I emailed Nora who advised I could collect it from the BDM office the same day, which I did. While my new pre-adoptive birth certificate was exactly as I'd been led to expect, it served to highlight that I now had five pre- and post-adoption birth certificates, all of which reflected incorrect details concerning my identity. One of them, the pre-adoptive birth certificate associated with the original registration of the birth of Georgia's baby, was actually correct. However, it was not officially connected to me, rather remained officially connected to Donna. By any measure, the situation was absurd.

The letter I received from BDM in May 2021 also advised that they were seeking further legal advice regarding the current status of my adoption. I followed this up at the end of May and again in June, emphasising that while BDM had recently requested this advice from the Victorian Government Solicitor's Office (VGSO), I had effectively been waiting a year to understand the legality of my situation—since the release of Donna's adoption records containing identifying information about Georgia, my putative Greek mother. I also emphasised that the government's legal advice was key to what needed to be requested of the County Court to fix my problem, which I was impatient to pursue and resolve.

On 29 June 2021, I subsequently received an email from Nora containing a "précis" of the VGSO's legal advice to her. It stated "the department's position" that, on the basis of the information provided to the County Court of Victoria at the time of my adoption, the information was correct, even though we now know it was incorrect, and therefore my adoption remained legally valid. Legally valid?! Really? The underlying message seemed to be that irrespective of how improper the circumstances of my adoption, irrespective of my misidentification, irrespective of whether it was accidental or intentional, the fact that an Adoption Order was granted in respect of me meant those circumstances were cleansed, laundered, legally papered over. Presumably, this was in line with how adoption was meant to solve the shame of birth outside marriage, too. But just ask Georgia how well that worked out. If I didn't already understand that adoption was legally draconian, on reading the "précis" it would have hit me like a tsunami. The DJCS's official legal position seemed to be more political than legal, elaborate spin for the purposes of damage control—it negated potential liability on the part of the Victorian Government but offered no justice for me. It didn't even acknowledge there was a problem and therefore laid the onus for fixing any problem that I identified squarely on my shoulders. Actually, more than elaborate spin, it felt like the ultimate official gaslight. I was beyond angry.

I immediately phoned Nora to request the grounds on which the VGSO's position was reached and she agreed to ask the VGSO if they could forward the details to me. I followed this up with an email to Nora outlining my concerns in relation to the matter. In particular, irrespective of whether my misidentification was accidental or intentional, I didn't understand why my adoptive parents' intentions were deemed to override my natural mother's intentions. Assuming AIS was correct and that Georgia Zagarelou was my natural mother, Georgia's intention as indicated by her signing the adoption consent form on 27 March 1963 was for another couple (Donna's adoptive parents) to privately adopt her baby (which was supposed to be me) in a privately arranged adoption, not for Lionel and Lois Mackieson (my adoptive parents) to adopt her baby in an adoption arranged through the Mission of St James and St John.[81] Ultimately, the key question, which I believed had significant implications for adoptions made under the current *Adoption Act 1984* as well as for my adoption made under the 1958 *Adoption Act,* was what circumstances, if any, would provide sufficient grounds to legally invalidate an adoption?

On 2 July, Nora advised me that the VGSO did not provide the full details of their advice to her originally, that the VGSO was reluctant to provide those details to me, and that BDM would meet with the VGSO on 5 July to discuss the matter. I emphasised that I needed to understand the grounds of the VGSO's position because it would determine my decision regarding what to do next. I also expressed that the Victorian Government may not consider it a big deal I was misidentified prior to being adopted but I did. On the basis that the Victorian Government's official legal position was essentially 'nothing to see here', I doubted BDM's capacity to pursue an application to the County Court that truly represented my best interests. I indicated to Nora that it increasingly seemed necessary for me to apply for discharge of my Adoption Order to

---

81   The Mission of St James and St John merged in 1997 with St John's Home for Boys and Girls and the Mission to the Streets and Lanes to form Anglicare Victoria, a non-government child and family welfare organisation.

be able to legally reclaim my true original identity and correct the historic records, that this was not only important for me but also for any other adopted individuals who may find themselves in a similar situation in future.

Nora contacted me on 5 July to advise that her meeting with the VGSO took place earlier that day as planned, and that the VGSO had advised her they were "not in a position to provide any further information," but would not explain why. I expressed my confusion; that it seemed to me the VGSO was hiding something, that I felt forced to seek the details of the VGSO's position through Freedom of Information (FOI) and seek my own independent legal advice; and that I would now consider making my own application to the County Court to discharge my Adoption Order and reclaim my true original identity. Nora contacted me again later the same day and relayed that the VGSO subsequently advised her they would not release further information because of "client privilege," whereby the DJCS was their client, not me. Really?! If so, why hadn't the VGSO told Nora that when she first asked for more information? The explanation itself—that I'm not "the client"—reinforced that I was considered under law merely the subject of an Adoption Order, not a party to it. I was apparently just an "adopted child" whose true identity didn't matter because the legal sanctity of the ancient and antiquated institution of adoption was the most important thing.

Two days later, Nora informed me that the VGSO had just sent her an email indicating they were willing to reconsider the details of my case. This was in response to her having forwarded to the VGSO my email to her of 29 June that outlined my concerns with the VGSO's legal position. Nora recognised that BDM's procedures didn't serve situations like mine well, and she said that BDM and the VGSO would meet the following week to discuss the matter further. On 13 July, Nora confirmed she had met with the VGSO again and that they were now reviewing my case, which was expected to take one to two weeks. In practice, it took a month for the VGSO to complete its review. Nora advised me of the outcome on 13 August, that the VGSO's initial advice stood. Why was I not surprised? Nora confirmed that making an application to the County Court appeared to be the only way I could legally identify Georgia as my mother. Indeed, I'd already worked out that pursuing such an application was the key to resolving the matter and achieving some peace of mind.

Meanwhile, I'd already contacted the County Court (on 7 July) to confirm the documents required for an application for Discharge of an Adoption Order and the lodgement fee (a substantial $500.50). I'd also met with AIS (on 26 July) to discuss my planned application to the County Court. I then drafted the documents for my application and, early the following month, engaged Macpherson Kelley solicitors to review and refine them.

I lodged the final version of my Application to Discharge my Adoption Order under s.19(1)(B) of the *Adoption Act 1984* with the County Court of Victoria on 13 August 2021. My application also sought for the Court to acknowledge my true pre-adoptive identity; to do all things necessary to amend the details on the relevant registers in accordance with my application; and to change my name from 'Penelope Kathleen Mackieson' to 'Penny xxx Zagarelou-Mackieson'.[82] It was a big thing for me to seek to change my legal name—the name I would thereafter be known by. As discussed in the first chapter of *Adoption Deception*, when Bruce and I got married in 1989 I couldn't embrace changing my family name to his. I couldn't accept having another identity change forced on me (i.e. in addition to the one forced on me through my adoption) simply because I had a new legal status. Just as then it was my choice to retain the name I had long been known by, it was

---

82 "xxx" represents the first name my Greek mother gave me, which I have chosen not to disclose here.

now my choice to change that name to reflect my true origins—my true maternal parentage, my parents' culture of origin, and my original name.

My application to the County Court thus aimed to legally reclaim and integrate my true original identity, as well as to correct my official records. Receipt of my application was confirmed by a Registrar of the Court on 24 August. The Registrar also indicated she would review the documents before forwarding them on to the Judge in charge of the Adoption and Parentage List.[83] The Registrar contacted me again on 28 September seeking clarification in relation to various aspects of my application, which she described as "very complicated." After several conversations, the Registrar confirmed she would now email AIS to request their report in relation to my application.

The next thing I heard in relation to my adoption discharge application was from AIS organising to meet with me on 11 October to discuss another option suggested by Her Honour Judge Davis, the Judge dealing with my application who had also dealt with my previous application to the County Court for release of identifying information about my putative Greek mother. Her Honour apparently accepted, even without direct DNA proof, that I am the person born xxx Zagarelou. However, she wondered whether I wished to simply correct and annotate the relevant records on the Birth and Adoption Registers under the provisions of section 20 and section 50 of the *Births, Deaths and Marriages Registration Act 1996*, rather than also discharge my Adoption Order which would necessarily change my legal identity, including my name and birth certificate.

The underlying messages seemed to be, firstly, that discharging my Adoption Order was an extreme response to my situation. Never mind that the granting of an Adoption Order was an extreme

---

83   See the County Court of Victoria's 'Adoption and Parentage' webpage.

measure in the first place. Secondly, that seeking to discharge their adoption was something only an adopted person who was unhappy with their adoptive family relationships would contemplate. Never mind that even as an archetypal 'well-adjusted adoptee' I'd long advocated to stop the practice of legally cancelling the adopted person's original identity on the granting of an Adoption Order. Certainly, I'd made statements in relation to my current Court application to the effect that I hadn't previously contemplated seeking discharge of my Adoption Order. But that was before it became clear there was no other way I could legally correct the mess created by my having been misidentified prior to my adoption. My situation was both extreme and messy, and dealing with it had derailed my life. I therefore resented tunnel-visioned thinking that undermined the validity of an adopted person who had positive relationships with their adoptive family wishing to reclaim their original identity, their birthright, their fundamental human right! But what could I really expect? Such thinking reflected the paternalism inherent in adoption law and practice, including the infantilising and demeaning nature of still being referred to as the "adopted child" throughout the *Adoption Act 1984*, despite now being an adult. Indeed, I was significantly older, more knowledgeable about the impacts of adoption, and more in tune with my own needs than were any of the parties directly or indirectly involved with my adoption when it was arranged. It was insulting and infuriating to still be treated as a child. I knew what I needed and what was best for me now, thanks very much!

I confirmed to AIS in our meeting that I wished the registers to be corrected and annotated as well as to proceed with my application to discharge my Adoption Order and integrate my pre-adoption and adoptive identities. The next day, I emailed the County Court indicating I had thoroughly read the relevant sections of the *BDM Act* as suggested by Her Honour and reiterated what I'd expressed to AIS the day before. For good measure, I also reiterated—as very clearly stated in the affidavit I submitted as part of my application—that my application had nothing to do with the quality of my relationships with my adoptive family.

My purpose for engaging Macpherson Kelley solicitors was two-fold: first, to review and refine my adoption discharge application documents, which had been completed; and second, to assist in seeking a formal apology from Monash Health for what happened to me at the QVMH and their destruction of my hospital records. In regard to the second purpose, my solicitor sent a letter to Monash Health at the end of September 2021 requesting a formal apology by close of business on 13 October 2021 for Monash Health's wrongful actions of the past and acknowledgement of the consequences. Monash Health's Chief Legal Officer responded the same day, expressing concern that the letter of request "accuses Monash Health of having engaged in conduct that is illegal" and inviting my solicitor "to clarify with precision the basis upon which it is alleged … that Monash Health committed any criminal offence."

My solicitor's reply to Monash Health included copies of the letter sent to AIS by Monash Health (in December 2020) in response to AIS's request for further information about what happened to the QVMH medical records for my mother and me, and the report prepared by AIS in relation to my first application to the County Court for release of identifying information about my real natural mother. My solicitor received a further reply from Monash Health's Chief Legal Officer on 21 October which advised that Monash Health had undertaken another thorough search of its records and was unable to find any further information than that previously provided. The letter also reiterated Monash Health's position that destruction of my medical records was permitted under the Public Record Office disposal schedule in place at the time they were "likely disposed of (in or around 1987)," and argued "there is no evidence that Monash Health has destroyed adoption records." No apology was offered. Rejected again.

It felt like Monash Health, just like the DJCS (aside from AIS) and the County Court, had treated me like a child, a silly child, who didn't understand how things worked. But I did know how things worked. I also had an idea how things should work, so I subsequently explored options for escalating the matter to hold Monash Health to account. This included consideration of administrative avenues, such as pursuing a complaint through the Health Complaints Commissioner, but I quickly dismissed that option. Based on a previous experience I knew that such a complaint, even if it met the relevant prerequisites, could be protracted and, in any event, was unlikely to achieve an outcome commensurate with the scale of negligence involved. My previous experience concerned the unexpected death of my adoptive mother in August 2011 from a toxic overdose of methotrexate, one of her prescribed medications for severe arthritis, which was incorrectly packaged by her pharmacy. In October 2011, I notified the Health Services Commissioner. They advised me that they were unable to assist due to a coronial investigation being undertaken to confirm the cause of Mum's death. So I then notified the Australian Health Practitioner Regulation Agency (AHPRA) to seek suspension of the responsible pharmacists' registrations.

The AHPRA investigations took some three-and-a-half years to finalise. They found that the principal pharmacist involved had "behaved in a way that constitutes unprofessional conduct" and that the other pharmacist had "behaved in a way that constitutes unsatisfactory professional performance." The principal pharmacist was subsequently "reprimanded," and conditions were imposed on both pharmacists' registrations "requiring [them] to be mentored for a period." That period was only 12 months. I pursued the matter as far as I could, but AHPRA deemed the appropriate response to the professional negligence that caused Mum's death to be a gentle slap on the respective pharmacists' wrists. Not only was there no justice for Mum, but the pharmacists remained free to continue working throughout the period of the investigations, free to continue their appalling practices in relation to the packaging of other elderly patients' medications. So, I had no faith that pursuing a complaint against the QVMH and Monash Health through an administrative body like the Health Complaints Commissioner would lead to any outcome other than more frustration and anger for me.

I therefore also explored the option of civil litigation, for which I was referred to a firm that specialises in personal injury and compensation claims. I had several discussions with a specialist lawyer who agreed there was a case to argue, despite there being no precedent in case law. Notwithstanding, I eventually decided against pursuing that pathway, too, because such cases are argued for the purpose of seeking financial compensation. This would have involved a psychiatric assessment to determine if I met the threshold of 10% impairment and, even if so, the assessment would have been challengeable by Monash Health. It was clear to me that the process itself would be challenging and would necessarily focus on my victimhood. I realised that I didn't want to be locked into a victim mentality for the duration of another, probably drawn-out, court process; that I just wanted to be able to heal and move on positively with the rest of my life.

The consultation process with the specialist lawyer helped me reaffirm that my aim was not to gain financially, and to clarify that what I really wanted was highly unlikely to be able to be achieved through litigation. What I really wanted was one of three components I'd identified as being essential to my healing—to receive a personal apology from Monash Health. The other two components were to achieve legal correction and integration of the facts underpinning my identity, which was in progress through my (second) County Court application; and to visit Greece to experience firsthand my country and culture of origin, a trip I knew I'd soon be able to re-plan with the easing of COVID-19 pandemic restrictions. They were all things over which I had some control—unlike having direct contact with my mother, which was at her behest. As the Kacey Musgraves song *Justified* rightly points out, "Healing doesn't happen in a straight line." Nor does healing happen to a schedule. In this context, I knew it was possible that achieving the latter two components may prove healing enough for me. But how would I know *until* they'd been achieved, especially as I had only so much influence over *when* they would be achieved? In the meantime it felt right to simultaneously continue pursuing an apology from Monash Health. It was important for me personally. As with many firsts, I knew it was also potentially important as a precedent for others who may find themselves in a similar situation to me in the future.

On 28 October 2021, AIS informed me that they'd received an official request from the County Court to provide a report in relation to my application, and that they'd also received a copy of my affidavit from the Court. Subsequently, we had a long meeting on 8 November as part of the process of AIS's preparation of their report. At last, things seemed to be moving along in relation to my County Court application. Monash Health remained a thorn in my side, but I began planning our trip to Greece (postponed from 2020) for July-August 2022. It hadn't occurred to me before then, but it now seemed possible that I could visit Greece with a new Australian passport. It was exciting to contemplate my first ever trip to my parents' homeland with my new integrated legal identity reflecting my Greek heritage.

2022: Healing

I remained too anxious about the resolution of my County Court application to focus on resuming Greek language lessons—that was serious work for someone like me who lacks aptitude for learning new languages. But I still felt optimistic that our long-awaited trip to Greece would be able to proceed. For orientation purposes, I decided to immerse myself in a week-long summer school on the 'History and culture of the ancient world' held from Monday 10 to Friday 14 January 2022 at the Hellenic Museum in Melbourne. The summer school was memorable for several reasons: the interesting stuff I learned about ancient Greece, the interesting people I met in the classes, the opportunity to thoroughly explore the Museum and, unexpectedly, Novak Djokovic's visa saga. Each morning after arriving by train at Flagstaff Station, I would emerge onto William Street to walk across to the Hellenic Museum. But first I had to pass through an angry crowd of Serbians out the front of the Office of the Registry of the High Court of Australia. They were protesting the Australian Government's decision to cancel Djokovic's visa to play at the 2022 Australian Open tennis tournament because of his unvaccinated status in relation to COVID-19. Inside our classroom, which was upstairs on the William Street side of the museum, even with the windows firmly shut and the microphone turned up, we often had to strain to hear our presenter, Dr Christopher Gribbin, over the megaphoned protestations on the opposite side of the street.

To be clear, I'm no Djokovic fan, I'm fully vaccinated, and I dislike sports stars and other celebrities being afforded special privileges. Nevertheless, I had some sympathy for Djokovic in relation to his visa saga. From my perspective, a government authority imposing on him something not necessarily in his own best interest, something that he wouldn't choose for himself, had parallels with forced adoption. Actually, around that time I could discern parallels with forced adoption in relation to many things, and with adoption generally in relation to most things. Patrick often said of me up until we actually departed for Greece that every sentence I uttered comprised "a noun, a verb, and adoption." Meanwhile, Bruce often described me as an "adoption jihadi." Neither portrayal was flattering, but I couldn't disagree. By then, adoption issues had been relentlessly front of mind for me for several years, and the mess associated with discovering I was swapped at birth before my adoption had only intensified my obsession—it was both involuntary and exhausting.

Early in February 2022, I began contacting the County Court regarding the progress of my adoption discharge application. On 3 February, I was informed that my application was before Her Honour and was asked whether I wished for the matter to be heard in chambers or at a hearing. I expressed my preference for a hearing, but only if it would not significantly delay resolution of the matter. On 14 February, I was informed that Her Honour was now reviewing my application. But before making any orders, Her Honour had invited Donna to make a submission within 14 days (by close of business 22 February 2022) regarding any objection she may have to an order by the Court for correction of the registers. Once again, I felt like someone else had been given the opportunity to deny my birthright. I had no idea how Donna would respond—I didn't know her, hadn't met her, and saw no reason to seek contact with her. I especially wanted to avoid the opportunity for Gwen and her family to potentially interpret any such outreach as me trying to interfere in Donna's relationships with them. Subject to receiving Donna's response, which I hoped would be positive if she responded at all, Her Honour was proposing to list the matter for a hearing to finalise the orders I sought. Well, that was something.

I contacted the County Court again on 23 February to check whether Donna had lodged any objection to the orders and, if not, whether a hearing had been scheduled. I emphasised that I'd booked overseas travel postponed from 2020 to depart Melbourne at the end of June 2022, and that I'd made the bookings under my proposed new legal name (boldly displayed in thick black writing on a yellow sticky label on our fridge), which I'd expected to have by now. It may have sounded pushy, but booking overseas travel under one name and changing it before travelling incurs substantial fees—the name details in one's passport must exactly match the name details under which one's international travel and accommodation is booked. I expressed to the Court that I was anxious for my application to be resolved as soon as possible so that I could apply for and receive my new passport in time. I contacted the Court again on 28 February. This time I was informed that the Court intended to hold a hearing remotely (over Zoom) and I was asked to indicate my availability the following week, which I did, but heard nothing back.

On 8 March, I contacted the County Court yet again to enquire whether a hearing had been scheduled. The next day the Court informed me that a Zoom hearing had been listed for midday on 15 March 2022. I was asked to confirm my availability and the name I wished to be legally known by, which I did. I understood that representatives from the DJCS, including AIS, would be in attendance and sought Her Honour's approval for some close family members (Bruce and Patrick, though Patrick ended up not attending) and friends (Veronica Sakell, Jenny McAuley, Catherine Neville, and Charlotte Smith), and a reporter (Gus McCubbing) to join the closed hearing.

In an ironic coincidence, the next day—10 March, my birthday—the Victorian Government tabled its response to the recommendations of the parliamentary *Inquiry into responses* to historical forced adoption in Victoria.[84] It also announced an allocation of more than $4 million in response to the inquiry, including to introduce "integrated birth certificates which include the names of both the adopted person's natural parents and their adoptive parents."[85] It was a bitter-sweet development. I'd advocated for years for integrated birth certificates but, even if already available in Victoria, the option of an integrated birth certificate would not help resolve the situation I found myself in.

2022: De-adoption

On 15 March 2022, in a hearing of the County Court of Victoria held via Zoom, Her Honour Judge Davis read out the reasons for her decision and then made orders in accordance with my application. Those orders discharged my Adoption Order; corrected the registrable information contained in the pre-adoptive entry in the register about my birth (so that my first and family names are recorded as 'xxx Zagarelou'[86] and my mother's name is recorded as 'Georgia Zagarelou'[87]); and changed my name from 'Penelope Kathleen Mackieson' to 'Penny xxx Zagarelou-Mackieson'. The Court also made orders of its own motion that corrected the registrable information contained in the pre-adoptive entry in the register about Donna's birth. The hearing was brief, no more than 15 minutes' duration, proceeded efficiently, and surprised me with how quickly it provided relief. My legal Adoption Order had been undone, reversed, cancelled. I was now de-adopted. I felt as if a giant yoke had been lifted from my shoulders, that I had been

---

84 See Victorian Government (2022) *Victorian Government Response to the Recommendations of the Legislative Assembly Legal and Social Issues Committee's Inquiry into Responses to Historical Forced Adoptions in Victoria.*
85 Quoted from Daniel Andrews and Jaclyn Symes (10 March 2022).
86 "xxx" represents the first name my Greek mother gave me, which I have chosen not to disclose here.
87 "Georgia" is an alias first name.

liberated. The physical sensation of lightness was extraordinary. Later that afternoon I walked to a local pub to meet Catherine for a celebratory champers and felt like I floated there—similar to how I felt after my meeting with AIS in June 2019 when they told me they'd identified my Greek mother, but without the haze. I was high even before my first sip of sparkling wine!

Later the same day, the County Court forwarded me copies of the orders made by Her Honour and advised that the Reasons for Decision would be provided in due course. On reading the orders—a Discharge of Adoption Order and a Correction of Registrable Information Order—my high quickly dissipated and my feet jolted annoyingly back to earth. I noticed an error on the Discharge of Adoption Order—it stated that I had filed the summons for the application on 20 August 2020, but the actual date was 13 August 2021. I advised the Court of the error the following day and, on 21 March, the Court sent me a corrected Discharge of Adoption Order. However, the date on the corrected order still indicated the wrong year, so once again I informed the Court. The next day the Court sent me a (second) corrected Discharge of Adoption Order. Later the same day, the Court sent me another (third) corrected Discharge of Adoption Order and a corrected Correction of Registrable Information Order because they'd noticed the wrong court reference number printed on both orders. This highlighted to me how easily mistakes can be made by people in positions of authority and how vigilant one must be in engaging with them. Whatever. It didn't seem like a very auspicious start to having my new legal identity.

On 25 March, I received a copy of Her Honour's Reasons for Decision and noticed another issue—the second point stated that I was "inadvertently swapped with another baby." However, both my investigations and those of AIS were unable to determine whether my having been swapped was accidental or intentional, which I'd made clear in my affidavit when addressing the destruction of relevant QVMH records. Therefore, for accuracy, I requested that Her Honour delete the word "inadvertently" from the official Reasons for Decision. On 31 March, I received an amended Reasons for Decision in accordance with my request.

Also on 25 March, I received a copy of my new birth certificate. I emailed Nora thanking BDM for the expeditious issuance of my new birth certificate and also raising the issue of two linked details that I considered should be corrected in accordance with the County Court orders. First, the birth registration number on my new birth certificate was the same as the number on the original/ pre-adoptive birth certificate for Gwen's baby. However, the Court found that I am not that person, rather that I am the person xxx Zagarelou, born to Georgia Zagarelou, who had a different original birth registration number. Second, the date of registration on my new birth certificate was the same birth registration date as for Gwen's baby, not for xxx Zagarelou, whose birth was registered on a different date in March 1963. I requested that these details be corrected and that my new birth certificate be re-issued accordingly.

Two days later I emailed Nora again, this time raising concerns with one of the two 'history notes' recorded on the back of my new birth certificate. To me, the note seemed highly confusing because it only captured details associated with BDM's corrections to my original birth and adoption registrations, rather than the actual circumstances that led to those administrative corrections. As such, I believed it could hinder me effecting my change of legal identity with relevant government and other institutions. I expressed that, while I understood the difficulty of comprehensively capturing the complexity of my situation in the history notes on the back of my birth certificate, if the real history couldn't be accurately represented there, I would prefer that no information be displayed at all.

Subsequently, on 31 March, I met with Nora O'Connor (BDM Registrar), John Tsitos (BDM Operations Manager) and Matthew

Reeder (Deputy Director, Adoption Services) to discuss the details to be printed on my new birth certificate. The various issues I'd raised were discussed and clarified and there seemed to be general agreement that my requests were reasonable. Then John carefully explained BDM's difficulties in implementing what I was requesting. As I understood it, BDM's electronic register was designed such that the individual is effectively attached to their birth registration record, rather than the birth registration record being attached to the individual. So, BDM couldn't simply un-attach the original birth registration details that had incorrectly been associated with Donna before her adoptive placement and attach them to me, or vice-versa—those details were too deeply embedded with our respective files. In other words, my new birth certificate could not have the birth registration number and date of registration recorded on my original birth record as lodged by my mother, Georgia Zagarelou, even though this is what would normally happen when an Adoption Order is discharged in Victoria.

I got the distinct impression that the departmental repre-sentatives were anxious about how I would respond to this problem. It would neither have surprised nor concerned me if they'd been briefed that I was demanding. I was focused on ensuring that only accurate details about me were recorded on my legal birth certificate and considered this to be a more than reasonable expectation, given the reason I'd sought to discharge my adoption in the first place. I also believed that my exceptional circumstances highlighted a bigger issue for BDM in relation to its electronic register that would be replicated numerous times as the misidentifications of other adopted individuals come to light in the future. But at that moment I was focused on finding an acceptable solution for my own case.

John tentatively suggested that the best way to proceed may be for BDM to re-register my birth from scratch. This meant that the date on which BDM re-registered my birth would become the new date of registration and that a completely new contemporaneous birth registration number would be assigned to me. Judging by John's face, he was surprised at how acceptable this option was to me. I figured it was appropriate to have a new birth registration, given I had a new legal identity. John further explained that, for BDM's purposes, the history notes would have to remain on the electronic register attached to my new birth registration record. However, when I pushed him on it he also indicated it was possible to withhold the second history note from being printed on the back of my birth certificate. Therefore, I requested that only the first history note be printed.

On 4 April, I received by express post my new legal birth certificate amended in accordance with the decisions we'd agreed at the meeting. Wow! At last the details recorded on my legal birth certificate were as accurate as they could be. So I immediately removed the yellow sticky label with my new name from the fridge and set about amending my driver's licence, bank account details, passport, etc. in accordance with my new legal identity. It was affirming and exciting to receive my new passport on 19 April, which was ultimately in plenty of time for our trip, though I'd paid a substantial fee to ensure expedited processing. I was finally getting somewhere—one of the three components I'd identified as essential to my healing had now been achieved.

Indeed, it was an achievement that Bruce was keen for us to celebrate. Initially, I wanted to wait until we'd been to Greece—the second of my three components of healing. But Bruce persuaded me that it was important to mark the occasion by holding a celebration sooner rather than later. So, we organised an event for 7 May 2022 for 50 family members and friends at Bahari, one of my favourite Greek restaurants in Melbourne, to celebrate formal recognition of my true origins and my new integrated legal identity. I enjoyed designing the invitation (included at Appendix I), organising the flowers, purchasing the table decorations (miniature Greek and Australian national flags), choosing the menu, and preparing the μπομπονιέρα[88] (pronounced 'bomboniéra') for our guests to take home. It was slightly stressful drawing up the invitation list, given the numbers were restricted to a maximum of 50 due to the size of the room at the venue. But by far the most difficult part of the preparations was drafting a speech explaining what I'd done and why I'd done it—the very reason we were celebrating. It wasn't that I lacked a clear understanding of my situation and responses or that I regretted my decisions in any way. Rather, having been immersed so deeply and for so long up until so recently in the complexities of it all, I was concerned that I wouldn't be able to explain it in a straightforward and coherent enough way to others who weren't up to speed on all the details.

It turned out to be a lovely event that was fully attended, aside from a small number isolating on the day because of COVID-19. Having agonised over the wording, I was relieved that my speech (included at Appendix II) seemed to go down well with our guests, too. The only hiccup was that I forgot to ensure everyone took their μπομπονιέρα—my friend Keri alerted me, but several guests had already left by that stage. (Coincidentally, it was Keri who noticed my PhD degree had been framed upside down after my conferral ceremony.) The significance of my milestone took some time to sink in, though I'd fully grasped it by the time we got together at Bahari and I was pleased that Bruce had pushed me to hold the celebration when we did.

In hindsight, coincidentally, holding such a celebration in May is auspicious in Greek culture: "According to Greek legend, the month of May has two meanings: the rebirth and death, but also the good and the bad."[89] Symbolically, our event farewelled

---

88 The Greek word for bomboniere.

89 Quoted from *The Greek Herald* (30 April 2021) 'What is the Custom of Protomagia (1 May) and Why Do Greeks Celebrate It?'.

my wrongly founded ('bad') identity and welcomed the integration of my true original ('good') identity, and celebrated the 'death' of Penelope Kathleen Mackieson and my 'rebirth' as Penny xxx Zagarelou-Mackieson. These interpretations may seem simplistic, but the parallels are pertinent given BDM ended up cancelling my 'original' birth registration and re-registering my birth to produce my new primary identity document. A long-time friend from our secondary school years, Jan Butterworth (nee Marshall), who attended our celebration summed things up beautifully with the gift of a poem that she lovingly penned (and illustrated) for me:

The Weaver—Penelope

Courageously she delicately unravels
the precious fabric
Discovering threads belonging elsewhere
she pauses her own work to take up that
of another
Determined and patient for completion
She hands over pieces for safe keeping
returning them to the moon and stars
Cautiously she resumes
re-weaving the fabric
keeping essentials
daring to add the flourish
And so the fabric emerges
Light and brilliance radiate from the cloth
As it was always meant to be.

Penny xxx Zagarelou-Mackieson

After the celebration, my focus turned primarily to our upcoming trip overseas. But I also further considered my third healing component—obtaining an apology from Monash Health—which I often discussed with close friends. One of those friends, Jenny, was my first manager when I joined the Victorian Government's child protection program in the Western Metropolitan Region of Melbourne in 1987. Jenny progressed to very senior roles in the department before her retirement, including one in which she worked with Andrew Stripp, the Chief Executive of Monash Health since 2016. Jenny very generously volunteered to make a personal approach to Professor Stripp to advocate for me, which she did in June 2022. They had a promising phone discussion, but Monash Health had not offered an apology by the time I headed overseas at the end of the month. I realised that I'd need to draw a line in the sand in regard to Monash Health at some stage but didn't feel that time had arrived just yet. I decided to see how I felt about it after returning from Greece before making the call on any further attempt to obtain an apology.

Bruce, Patrick and I departed Melbourne for Scotland on 27 June. We stayed in Edinburgh for two weeks in the same accommodation, so that we'd be well-rested and relaxed after the long journey from Australia and as ready as we'd ever be for our first trip to Greece. During our first week in Edinburgh, I travelled solo by train to London while Bruce and Patrick played golf at St Andrews. Golf isn't my thing and being in the UK was too good an opportunity to miss meeting in person my new friend, Gonda Van Steen, who I'd reached out to in 2020 during the first COVID-19 lockdown in Victoria. We had only a small window of opportunity while in the UK, as it was the end of the university semester and Gonda and her husband were packing up Gonda's rental flat in London before heading home to the USA. It was lovely to meet and spend time with them, and I very much appreciated their generosity in taking time out and having me stay in the midst of their moving.

Gonda (pronounced 'Honda') is a Professor at King's College London, where she holds the Koraes Chair of Modern Greek and Byzantine History, Language and Literature, and is Director of the Centre for Hellenic Studies. Gonda is fluent in five languages, including English and Greek. Gonda is also author of *Adoption, Memory, and Cold War Greece: Kid pro quo?* (2019), a book about the post-war adoptions of more than 3,000 Greek children into the USA, which accelerated after the Greek Civil War and during the global Cold War. Having read her book, I emailed Gonda asking if she knew whether Greek babies had been similarly adopted into Australia. Gonda promptly replied in the negative from which we established a warm ongoing email exchange and friendship. I learned from Gonda that the first place she ever visited in Greece was the town where my mother, Georgia, has resided since returning to Greece in the early 1970s. Gonda learned from me that one of the Greek-American adoptees referred to in her book is a distant cousin of mine, identified through AncestryDNA.

2022: Greekification

On 12 July, Bruce, Patrick and I departed Edinburgh on an overnight flight to Athens. We stayed in the Greek capital two nights which, as I'd hoped, served as a great introduction to Greece. We took in several historic sites and, in particular, appreciated the magnificence of the Acropolis. Having arrived early in the morning at our centrally located accommodation aptly named The Athens Gate Hotel, we headed upstairs to its rooftop restaurant for our first breakfast in the country. Rather sleepily, we stepped out of the lift to suddenly and unexpectedly behold the Acropolis set high on its rocky plateau. The view was gobsmackingly spectacular and quite literally took our collective breath away.

Down at ground level, Athens was very hot and the air very still, hovering around 40C each day. There were bushfires on the city outskirts while we were there and, even with my minimal Greek language skills, it was obvious from the saturation TV coverage that the fires were burning destructively out of control in several areas. Nevertheless, our pre-planned hire car journey to Nafplio in the Peloponnese wasn't affected. With Bruce at the wheel and Patrick and I navigating from maps apps on our mobile phones, we somehow managed the most difficult part of the drive quite smoothly. That is, we exited Athens without any arguments (in contrast, we'd had a few surprisingly heated exchanges driving around Scotland) and without having to make any hard left-hand turns, about which we'd been quite concerned given the switch to driving on the opposite (right-hand) side of the road and in less orderly conditions than we were used to. The rest of the drive to Nafplio was quite relaxing, as it was mostly on good quality freeways that were apparently funded by the European Union for the 2004 Olympics, though not completed until some years later.

Our accommodation during our week in Nafplio—a very comfortable two-bedroom apartment with three balconies, views of the water, and a rare off-street carpark—was descriptively named on Booking.com as "Quiet luxury apartment near city center and port." The apartment was located only a 10-minute walk from the city centre. So, despite the weather conditions that were even hotter than they'd been in Athens, we were able to walk into town each day and enjoy the numerous historic sites, tourist attractions, docks and marinas, beaches, shops and restaurants. One day we also drove, again mostly via freeway, to the small village where Georgia grew up—it was similar in size to the tiny town in which I grew up in eastern Victoria. Another day we drove to the beachside town where Georgia and Nikos live. While there, Bruce insisted that we visit the business we believed Nikos operated, and recognised Nikos and his sons from their Facebook photos. I was equally insistent that we shouldn't attempt to introduce ourselves, especially as it was immediately clear they didn't speak English. As far as we knew, Nikos had no idea I even existed, and I felt it was totally inappropriate to try and communicate in the middle of his workplace in the midst of the tourist season that I was his 'secret sister' from Melbourne. Bruce kept reminding me that we didn't know when, or even if, we'd ever visit Greece again. But I felt acutely uncomfortable, more than a fly on the wall, a spy, and although slightly tempted, I stuck firm to my decision not to engage with Nikos. Regardless, it was an idyllic Greek town with a fabulous beach, sensational views, and quality eateries. It was also priceless to experience the place where my mother and one of my brothers lived. I took the time to choose some smooth pebbles from the beach to bring home as a constant reminder that I was actually there.

On 20 July, Bruce, Patrick and I drove back from Nafplio to Athens. Bruce and Patrick delivered me very close to my new digs, Central Athens Studios, then battled their way out of the chaotic central city traffic to return our hire car to the airport and catch their flight home to Melbourne. I enjoyed a busy few days by myself visiting the Acropolis, numerous other ancient sites and the Acropolis Museum, as well as shopping for locally designed and made clothing, jewellery and gifts. I was then joined by my friend, Catherine. Our favourite activity at the end of each long hot day was relaxing at a different rooftop bar with a view of the Acropolis while sipping cocktails and watching the sun set. Catherine found the Acropolis as mesmerising as I did, despite that visiting the ancient site in the plus-40C heat was highly challenging. We departed Athens by ferry for Parikia, the capital, largest town and busiest port on the island of Paros, renowned for its fine white marble. We were joined there a few days later by two more friends, Veronica and her husband Bruce Gemmell, before the four of us embarked on a nine-day chartered yacht cruise around the Small Cyclades group of islands within the Cycladic Archipelago in the Aegean Sea.

The cruise could not have been more relaxing. Under the gentle guidance of our fabulous skipper, Anthony (Antonis), we criss-crossed the Cyclades and lolled about the Aegean Sea, anchoring wherever the conditions pleased and swimming off the boat whenever the mood took us. We harboured at idyllic coastal villages, dined at their local tavernas and swam at their pretty sand and pebble beaches. The views were consistently picturesque and the ambience unfailingly inviting and laid back. In every village, traditional whitewashed houses with flat rooves and blue-painted doors, window shutters and frames, and neat stone-cobbled paths highlighted by broad white grout, replicated those at Parikia. In the same way, the islands themselves—typically dry, hilly, rocky and minimally treed with low-growing shrubs—replicated Paros. Our spontaneous cruise itinerary included Aliki, a fishing village on the southwest of Paros which features a wide, protected beach; Antiparos, a small island which closely neighbours Paros to the south-west and features picture-postcard windmills and vivid bougainvillea-adorned houses and shops; Iraklia, a small mountainous island south-east of Paros which has been inhabited from early antiquity and features caves, rock paintings and fortress ruins; Koufonisia, a community of three main islands north-west of Iraklia which have been inhabited since prehistoric times; Naxos, the largest Cycladic island, which neighbours Paros to the east and where, according to Greek mythology, Zeus was raised in a cave; and Schoinousa, a small island south of Naxos and north-east of Iraklia, also inhabited since antiquity and featuring several Greek, Roman and medieval sites of archaeological interest.

On returning to Paros at the end of the cruise, Veronica and Bruce headed off to visit Veronica's paternal extended family in the province where her father was born and raised before he emigrated to Australia—coincidentally, that province neighbours the one where Georgia resides. Meanwhile, Catherine and I ferried to Santorini, a Southern Aegean island in an active volcanic area south of Paros and the Small Cyclades, for a few days. On Santorini, we stayed in Fira, a traditional cliffside town that closely resembles

Oia—the archetypal picture-postcard town with flat-roofed, white-washed houses, blue-painted church domes and windmills that is used extensively in tourist promotions for Greece. In fact, we had spectacular views of Oia from our respective rooms and agreed that photos do not, cannot, do it justice. Unfortunately, Santorini's magical ambience would become somewhat disturbed by about 11.00 am each morning when Fira became packed with tourists day-tripping from the massive ocean liners constantly harbouring below the cliffs. From Santorini, Catherine and I flew back to Athens on 10 August and left for Melbourne the same day.

I found it very hard to leave Greece (as did Catherine, too), having loved each and every part of my trip. I loved exploring and absorbing the ambience of the ancient archeologically-rich city of Athens, first with Bruce and Patrick, later solo, and then with Catherine. I loved the week with Bruce and Patrick in Western Greece based mainly in the ancient coastal city of Nafplio, and driving around visiting places that I knew were of significance to my mother. I loved the rejuvenating experience of the chartered yacht cruise with Catherine, Veronica and her Bruce, enjoying the beauty, simple delights, and relaxation associated with sailing around the Aegean islands. And I loved the final few days with Catherine on the spectacular, though considerably more "touristical", as Anthony would say, island of Santorini. It wasn't so much that I didn't want to go home to Australia, to my life in Melbourne, more that I felt I could easily have stayed indefinitely in Greece. I felt very comfortable there, everywhere I went, and slotted into the Greek coffee, food, and pace of life as if I'd grown up with it. Before I'd left for Greece, people, especially Greek-Australian friends and acquaintances, told me that I'd see many people there who looked like me, that I'd blend in like a local. I'd hoped and dreamt that they'd be right and, indeed, they were! Not only did I see many familiar-looking faces for the first time in my life, but I came away from Greece feeling securely anchored. The trip was an unexpected overachievement in terms of my second identified component of healing.

It didn't take much to scratch the surface, either. Greeting service staff with a friendly Γεια σας (pronounced "Geia sas" and translates literally to "Hello you") or thanking them with a polite Ευχαριστώ (pronounced "Efcharistó") would often elicit a stream of friendly Greek conversation because they expected me to know what they were saying. I usually responded in English but a few people, especially in Nafplio, still commented that they thought I seemed Greek. To my ears, this was the ultimate compliment! Occasionally, when I had time and there was no one else around, I would explain that my parents were Greek but I had only recently discovered this. Invariably my disclosure drew a reciprocal disclosure about a secret recently uncovered in their own family. For example, someone's middle-aged uncle had recently discovered he had another child who was conceived prior to his marriage. The child, now an adult, found their father through a consumer genetic genealogy test (go figure!) and was subsequently embraced by their father and his family. Another example was a man's wife who was told as a young adult that she was adopted as a small baby by her aunt and uncle in Greece and grew up believing that they were her parents. Accordingly, she also grew up believing that her natural parents in Australia were her aunt and uncle and that their children were her cousins, although they were in fact her full siblings. She was, understandably, angry for years afterward. Indeed, there was no shortage of adoption stories, including reunions, that local Greek people volunteered in conversation with me. Similarly, people who needed to check my passport sometimes noted that Zagarelou was a Greek name and would ask about my heritage, what part of Greece my family were from, and engage in further conversation about it.

Despite the fact that I was adopted and raised in Australia by non-Greeks, didn't know my Greek natural family members, hadn't previously visited Greece or learned much Greek language, I felt like the Greek people I met in Greece embraced me and made me feel very welcome there. In turn, I felt a real connection to Greece, I felt at home there just as much as I feel at home in Australia. These feelings have stayed with me since coming home. Indeed, I would describe my experience of Greece as a perfect balm for my soul—it was restorative and healing, and has helped me reset both psychologically and physically. In fact, I left Melbourne with chronically painful knees, especially the left one, which I originally injured when I was 15. The pain came upon me suddenly and inexplicably in September 2019, like I'd imagine from a sharp knife stabbing deep into the knee joint. The nature and degree of pain was way higher than my doctors could fathom from the results of an MRI scan, which showed general wear-and-tear associated with my age and sporting activities in younger life. There was some arthritis in my knees and hips, but not enough to generate the sharp radiating pain that often also affected my hips and gait and, when acute, kept me awake at night. Even during our fortnight in Edinburgh, I had a couple of bad nights with pain and ended up sleeping on a sofa in the lounge room with my legs and knees propped up by cushions. Yet by the time I left Greece, I'd forgotten all about the pain because there was none, it had disappeared altogether.

My theory is that I'd become so desirous of visiting Greece and so worried I wouldn't be able to get there that I locked the tension in my body. My left knee was probably the most vulnerable location for my anxiety to latch on to. I dislocated the kneecap playing netball at 15, and it was problematic throughout my late teens and early adulthood whenever I played sport or exercised (i.e. it was prone to swelling, inflammation and pain that impacted my mobility afterwards). Eventually, after spending thousands on physiotherapy treatment, in my late 20s I had surgery on the knee and a large piece of torn cartilage (meniscus) was removed. It felt much better afterward, though it has since been grindy and still prone to swelling and inflammation. Anyway, by the end of my month in Greece, I was obviously no longer anxious about visiting my parents' homeland—I was there! So, my theory goes, that my body was able to release the tension I was holding and the acute pain associated with it. While in Greece I apparently swapped my knee pain for a Mediterranean suntan, something I never expected to be able to acquire because I'd long believed I had pale Celtic-Anglo skin.

My only regret in regard to visiting Greece is that I didn't visit years earlier. I had travelled to various European countries, some several times, earlier in my adulthood before I knew about my Greek heritage. I would most definitely have chosen to visit Greece if I'd known my true ancestry when I began my quest in 1989 to piece together my pre-adoptive identity. This was brought home to me a few days after I arrived home from Greece while watching a TV show on SBS, *Treasures of Greece*. The presenter, Bettany Hughes, said simply, "Greece is a tapestry." It made complete sense that my life should replicate Greece herself, that my life is a tapestry, too. But my tapestry still had some big holes in it, especially in relation to connecting with my natural family, as well as a few loose ends in relation to dealing with having been swapped at birth. Having now been to Greece, my first priority back in Melbourne was to resume work on the biggest hole. So I met with AIS on 25 August, gave feedback on our visit to my brother Nikos's business, and requested that AIS outreach directly to him there. AIS subsequently prepared a letter in Greek and sent it to Nikos at his business address.

While waiting for the letter to arrive in Greece and, hopefully, for a response from Nikos, I followed up a loose end. I realised that my focus in relation to my missing records had been on Monash Health because the QVMH had merged with it in 1987. But there were other relevant records—client records held by the legal firm that arranged the private adoption of Georgia's baby. In 1990, McKean Park Lawyers acquired the legal firm that had, in turn, acquired the legal firm of the solicitor who obtained Georgia's consent for her baby's adoption in 1963. I contacted McKean Park Lawyers early in September 2022 seeking copies of any records relating to Georgia, my birth and my adoption that may have been held by the firm. They replied promptly, advising that any paper file containing information about my adoption would have been destroyed after six years from the date of the merger that took place in 1982. Oh, well. It was worth a try.

2022: An apology

My focus returned to Monash Health once again. I decided after all to make a final attempt to obtain an apology and, should it fail, to resume counselling with a view to working through my frustration and disappointment and hopefully achieve closure in relation to the matter. Therefore, on 15 September, I sent a two-page letter (included at Appendix III) to the Chair and Directors of the Board of Monash Health requesting a formal apology for wrongs done to me at the QVMH in 1963. Namely, that I was separated from my mother in coercive circumstances for the purpose of adoption ('forced adoption') and misidentified (swapped with another baby) prior to my adoptive placement at three weeks of age. As a gesture of good faith, I indicated that I had decided to not further pursue the matter of the wrongful destruction of my mother's and my QVMH records. I also highlighted that this was my third request for such an apology from Monash Health and that I was not seeking financial compensation.

Two months after sending my letter I received a brief letter of apology from Professor Andrew Stripp on behalf of the Chair and Directors of the Monash Health Board (included at Appendix

IV). My friend Jenny's personal approach to Professor Stripp must have facilitated a formal response after all. In any event, I had to read the letter several times and consider it carefully for a couple of days before I could verbalise my thoughts and feelings about it. Overall, the apology was "formal, written and genuine," as I'd requested. It also offered deep, in fact "deepest" regret, as I'd requested. But what the apology did not do was "acknowledge full and unconditional responsibility" for my having been coercively separated from my mother for the purpose of adoption, for my having been misidentified, and for the harms inflicted on me as a consequence. Thus I found the apology underwhelming but sincere, less than I asked for but probably as much as I expected. I appreciate that Monash Health's Chief Legal Officer would have trawled through the letter for the purposes of damage control—to minimise any potential for a future financial compensation claim in relation to that big bogey for maternity hospitals, forced adoption. That would account for the omission of any reference to the coercive circumstances of my adoption. Nevertheless, if the redress scheme promised by the Victorian Government for mothers affected by forced adoption between 1958 and 1984[90] is ever extended to also include the people who, as babies, were forcibly separated from their mothers for the purpose of adoption, who knows? I might consider making an application through the redress scheme down the track. Still, I accepted the written apology from Monash Health in the spirit it was intended—to facilitate my healing and enable me to move on. And I have been able to move on.

---

90   See Daniel Andrews and Jaclyn Symes (10 March 2022). Op. cit.

2022: Connecting with my maternal family

On 4 October 2022, Ange phoned to inform me, first, that there had as yet been no response from Nikos to the letter AIS sent to his business address in Greece. Ange agreed to follow up with a phone call directly to Nikos, as she had his mobile phone number. Second, there had apparently been a change in BDM policies during the previous six months concerned with verifying an individual's existence, subsequent to which AIS was now able to release to me information about a third maternal sibling that I hadn't known about. Georgia and her husband had had not two, but three, children in their marriage: two sons, my brothers Nikos and Yiannis, and then a daughter, my sister Sofia.[91] Just like me and the boys, Sofia was also born here in Melbourne before her parents returned to Greece with her and her two brothers. Wow! Completely out of left field, this was mind-blowing information about my maternal family—another jackpot! It was very exciting having another sibling! Another beautiful thread to weave into the tapestry of my identity.

On 6 October, Ange informed me that she'd spoken directly in Greek with Nikos at his business in Greece. Nikos told Ange he hadn't yet received her letter. More importantly, he also indicated that he is not the Nikos who is my brother, rather a paternal cousin of the same name. Phew! I was so relieved that I'd stuck to my guns and not tried to communicate directly with Nikos when we visited his business. It would have added an extra layer of confusion, as well as inadvertently disclosing private (and secret) information about his aunt Georgia's adopted child. Ange, likewise, did not disclose any such information to cousin Nikos—early in their conversation when she was confirming his identity Nikos had immediately indicated that Georgia was not his mother but his aunt. Cousin Nikos subsequently provided Ange with my brother

91   "Sofia" is an alias first name.

Nikos's mobile phone number, to which she sent a text message in Greek requesting that he contact her.

On 11 October, Ange contacted me again to advise that the previous night she'd had a 15-minute phone conversation directly in Greek with my brother, Nikos. Cousin Nikos had received AIS's letter since her previous phone call—he reportedly didn't open the letter but gave it directly to his cousin/my brother, Nikos. Ange informed my brother Nikos that there was someone in Melbourne AIS strongly believed was his older sister, that I was named xxx by his mother but was now known as Penny. Nikos was reportedly gobsmacked but also open and accepting of the information Ange provided about me. Ange said she explained to Nikos that she hadn't discussed any of this with his cousin Nikos, but that she had spoken with his mother, Georgia, several times and that Georgia had consistently indicated she wanted no further contact from Ange or any contact from me. Ange also explained to Nikos that she was contacting him because he and his siblings have a right to know they have an older sister.

Ange said my brother Nikos did not speak to her in English but he did understand the English term 'DNA'. When Ange explained that I recently discovered I'd been misidentified before my adoption, Nikos also understood why it was important for genetic verification of our relationship. He indicated he would consider DNA testing and was curious whether we also shared the same father. Wow! Me, too! Nikos requested that Ange phone him again in two weeks' time, as he had much to consider and discuss with his two younger siblings in the interim. It was all absolutely wonderful news! It really felt like things were progressing in relation to connecting with my maternal family. I crossed my fingers and tried hard not to hold my breath until Ange next spoke with my brother Nikos.

I informed Claire Forster of these developments, and she was excited for me, too. EFHAS had been unsuccessful in identifying and engaging any of my close relatives but remained committed to telling my story. To this end, Claire requested my permission, Ange's and the Department's to film me receiving the update from Ange (remotely via Teams) following her two-week follow up phone call to my brother Nikos. Ange consented to her voice being recorded, subject to formal approval by the DJCS. Claire subsequently travelled from Perth and, with a locally-recruited crew, filmed me over three days from 24–26 October 2022.

The EFHAS filming included one-on-one interviews with two experts relevant to my circumstances. The first of these took place on 25 October with medical historian Dr Madonna Grehan.[92] Madonna explained how easy it would have been for babies to be misidentified at the QVMH during the era in which I was born because of the identification practices in place at the time. In the 'Labour Ward', as it was then called, each newly delivered baby had their mother's family name, their date of birth, and their sex handwritten with a fountain pen in Indian (indelible) ink on a thin brown cardboard luggage tag, which was attached to their wrist by a length of brown string tied in a bow. This reinforced my mental image of babies identified for adoption being treated like packages sorted into pigeon-holes, as evoked by the photo (in Chapter 1) of nurses at the QVMH tending to at least 20 newborns tucked neatly into conjoined cribs. Before each baby was moved into the nursery, the tag was removed while they were bathed and then a new tag—comprising a length of woven cotton tape on which the baby's family name and date of birth was again handwritten with a fountain pen using Indian ink—would have been stitched on to their wrist. The handwriting on the tag could be difficult to read at the best of times, but a cardboard tag could also get wet and the writing on a cotton tape band could also be poorly situated or

---

92 See the University of Melbourne's Faculty of Medicine, Dentistry and Health Sciences' entry, 'Nursing: Dr Madonna Grehan' (2022).

stitched in a way that made the name even harder to read. A brown string bow could be undone by the baby's own wriggling arms and hands, or the cotton tape could become loose and fall off through the baby's invariable weight loss after birth. These problems were apparently commonplace, happening on a daily basis, and where they happened to two babies lying beside each other, the risk of misidentification would have been high. Madonna's description supported the theory that my misidentification—having been switched with Donna—was probably accidental, rather than intentional. It also supported my theory that there were probably many such misidentifications.

Most interestingly, Madonna also informed me that, in 1992, Monash Health commissioned her to undertake a research project through which she discovered 18 months' worth of QVMH medical records had inexplicably been destroyed without first having gone through the standard cataloguing process. The period relating to the destroyed records included all of 1963, early 1964, and possibly also late 1962. This means Monash Health has, in fact, known since 1992 that the QVMH medical records for the period of my birth and hospital stay were summarily destroyed, inappropriately even according to its own practices, and for no apparent reason. This information clarified for me why other people born at the QVMH and adopted around the same years as I was had been able to access their medical records but I could not. However, it also fuelled the mystery regarding the destruction of the QVMH medical records for 1963. Why hadn't Monash Health been up-front with me about this? Was it really some sort of cover up, after all?

The second one-on-one interview took place on 26 October with Jason Reeve from AncestryDNA. I was told that Brad Argent would have conducted the interview but he was in the UK at the time. Jason updated me on my 'DNA Relatives' matches and ethnicity results. He advised that, although there were still no close matches, the results for my distant matches were consistent with Georgia being my true natural mother. This information was reassuring, regardless of whether any of my three siblings in Greece agreed to do a DNA test. Jason also advised me that improved analysis now showed I have no Italian heritage whatsoever—it had been unpacked into heritage originally from other parts of Greece and other nearby countries of Europe; and strong heritage from the region of Greece where my mother is from (consistent with the results from my 23andMe test in 2018).

The best interview filmed by EFHAS, however, was my Teams meeting with Ange on 26 October when she advised me about separate phone calls she'd had the previous day with each of my brothers, Nikos and Yiannis, in Greece. Ange spoke first with Nikos, as they'd agreed. Nikos explained that the siblings had, for various reasons, delegated Yiannis to engage with her (and me). Meanwhile, the siblings had not yet discussed the matter with their mother. Regardless, Yiannis expressed that all three were very excited to have another sister, that they weren't expecting this to happen to their family but they were open-minded and non-judgmental, that they embraced me, and that they were very excited and happy to proceed with DNA testing as soon as possible to clarify our relationships before we meet! This news was simply amazing! It exceeded my best-case scenario exponentially. I was overjoyed, emotional and teary, all caught on camera, of course! Knowing Brad Argent's commitment to assisting me, Claire volunteered AncestryDNA to send test kits to my siblings in Greece and expedite the processing of the tests.

Still, the DNA testing process for my siblings was neither straightforward nor speedy. There were logistical issues with DHL delivering the DNA test kits from Ancestry in the UK to Yiannis in Greece, followed by communication issues in relation to the accompanying instructions, which were written only in English and not in Greek. Eventually, a bilingual genetic genealogist from Athens was engaged to visit my siblings to facilitate the testing process and subsequently send the samples to the AncestryDNA lab in Ireland. But there was another logistical hiccup with DHL in Greece initially refusing to transport the test samples, apparently because they contained biological substances. D'oh! The entire consumer genetic genealogy testing industry has evolved sending human spittle mixed with a stabilising solution in plastic tubes through the post!

Weeks, then months, passed. Once again, it was a process over which I had no control. In some ways, it was just another delay, another indeterminate period of waiting for the next twist or turn on the ridiculous roller coaster ride of my life. Given my mother's spirited refusal communicated through AIS to engage with me, I'd had no expectation that my siblings would be willing to do so. But despite the unexpectedness of their willingness, it was difficult for my mind to not gallop ahead. My anticipation of directly engaging with my brothers and sister in Greece was equal parts tantalising and torturous. Logically, I knew that the key to the next chapter of my life was obtaining the DNA proof of our relationships. I was confident that the results would show we were probably half-siblings or, less likely but still possible, full siblings. Still, I felt I had no choice but to wait for the results, even though my heart was impatient. I steadfastly refused to accept my siblings' contact details and engage with them while there was any chance, no matter how small, that we were not related after all. I felt the need to protect myself and everybody else involved. I was determined to not go through what I'd been through with my wrongly identified maternal family all over again.

2023: Wow!

By January 2023, I was also impatient for my second trip to Greece, regardless of the timing or outcome of my siblings' DNA test results. So, I began planning for a trip to Greece in April-May with two close friends: Catherine, who had joined me on my first trip, and Jenny, who'd never been to Greece and was very keen to visit. Bruce and Patrick had made it amply clear that they would be very happy to visit Greece with me again, especially to meet my family members, but that they were not at all keen to make the long-haul flight involved within less than a year of their first trip to Greece. Whatever. I had something to plan for and look forward to with my friends, something within my control.

Eventually, on 8 March 2023, Jason Reeve from AncestryDNA informed me—in person and in front of the EFHAS cameras—of the results of the AncestryDNA tests taken by two of my putative siblings in Greece. Apparently, my third putative sibling was unavailable to take a test on the day it was arranged with the genetic genealogist for them to be done. Notwithstanding, the results from the two tests taken confirmed that we are maternal half-siblings! The relief of it all! At last, I could breathe again.

At last, I could shift my focus to getting to know my maternal siblings before arriving in Greece at the end of April, by then only a month-and-a-half away. To this end, on 15 March, I had my first phone conversation with my brother Yiannis in Greece, facilitated by Ange who also translated for us. Yiannis spoke in Greek and sounded as excited and relieved as me to learn the news about the DNA test results. He expressed that our other two maternal siblings were also very excited, welcoming, and looking forward to meeting me on my upcoming trip to Greece. It was very reassuring. Yiannis also indicated that the three siblings wished to tell our mother that they now knew her secret and that they have embraced me. He said they were determined I would meet our mother on this trip.

On 26 March, I had a second phone conversation with Yiannis, again facilitated by Ange, and in the meantime Yiannis and I had exchanged emails and a few photos. Yiannis expressed his opinion that we all looked a lot like our mother, though I was still not convinced that I did. Yiannis undertook to arrange a further phone conversation with our other siblings.

On 2 April, without any translation assistance from Ange, Bruce and I had our first face-to-face conversation on Viber with Yiannis and Sofia, who spoke good English. I was deeply moved when Sofia expressed her delight in discovering that she had a sister, something she had apparently always longed for, and that she was amazed by my facial likeness to our mother, especially to how Georgia looked a few years ago. We tentatively planned to meet up in Athens before heading to their local town and spending more time together there. I couldn't wait to see my siblings in person, to be able to take in their expressions and mannerisms, as well as their faces. Bruce and I got the strongest impression that they couldn't wait to meet me in person, too.

It felt like the beginning of a completely new chapter in my life, a chapter I would never have imagined. I had just turned 60 and was about to visit the country where I was conceived, my country of origin, for the second time in less than twelve months. I was about to meet my maternal siblings for the first time in our lives and, maybe, I was also about to meet my mother for the first time since my birth. Wow!

CHAPTER 4

There's a Greek Story Behind Everything

The origins of many aspects of contemporary western culture can be traced back to Ancient Greek culture, which thrived over two thousand years ago. Many areas of study—such as astrology, biology, engineering, linguistics, mathematics, and medicine—are based on foundations laid by brilliant thinkers of ancient Greece.[93] Greek-American character Gus Portokalos's proud claim in the hit romantic comedy, *My Big Fat Greek Wedding*, "Give me a word … and I'll show you that the root of that word is Greek,"[94] is well-founded as well as humorous. Many English words—perhaps more than 150,000—are derived from Greek words.[95] This includes everyday words like 'alphabet', formed from the first two letters of the Greek alphabet (pronounced 'alpha' and 'beta'), as well as medical, scientific, and technical terms. Even the variants of the

---

93 See Toni Hetherington's article, 'How Greek Mythology Continues to Have a Large Influence on Our Modern Lives' (14 May 2019).
94 Quoted from Katerina Daley (9 August 2022) 'My Big Fat Greek Wedding: 10 Most Iconic Quotes'.
95 See Martha Peraki and Catherine Vougiouklaki's article, 'How Has Greek Influenced the English Language?' (18 May 2015); and the Centre of Excellence's article, 'Why Greek Mythology is Still Relevant' (2 September 2022).

SARS-CoV-2 virus that causes COVID-19 have been named using the letters of the Greek alphabet.[96]

References to ancient Greek mythology are also deeply embedded in western culture. For example, baby names, including my adoptive first name, *Penelope* (the wife of the Greek hero, *Odysseus*), and *Troy* (the ancient Greek city); company brand names, like the sporting goods company, *Nike* (the Greek goddess of victory), and the luxury goods company, *Hermès* (the emissary and messenger of the Greek gods); place and facility names, such as Tasmania's *Mount Olympus* (the home of the gods and the site of the throne of *Zeus*, god of the sky), and the Royal Australian Navy's training facility in Victoria, *Cerberus* (the multi-headed dog that guarded the gates of the underworld); planet names, including the seventh planet from the sun in our solar system, *Uranus* (the personification of the sky and a primordial deity in Greek mythology); and logos, such as the symbol for medicine and the medical profession (the snake-entwined staff of *Asklepios*, the Greek god of healing[97]) and the University of Melbourne's coat of arms[98] (which features a depiction of the Greek goddess, *Nike*, as Winged Victory[99]); and so on.

Adoption is no exception. For most of my life I've known that modern western adoption is also derived from an institution developed in ancient Greece. Findings from recent archaeological and genetic research suggest that living Greeks are descended from Mycenaeans.[100] So I may well be descended from the Mycenaean ancestors idealised by the ancient Greeks in their "epic poems and

---

96 See Kathy Katella's article, 'Omicron, Delta, Alpha, and More: What to Know About the Coronavirus Variants' (17 November 2022).

97 See *Theoi.com*'s entry for 'Asklepios' (2017); Toni Hetherington (2019). Op. cit.; and the World Health Organization's 'The WHO Logo and Emblem' (2022).

98 See the University of Melbourne Library's webpage, 'Winged Victory Coat of Arms, University of Melbourne' (2017).

99 See the Wikipedia entry, 'Nike (Mythology)' (2022).

100 See Ann Gibbons' article, 'The Greeks Really Do Have Near-Mythical Origins, Ancient DNA Reveals' (2 August 2017).

classic tragedies."[101] This realisation prompted me to learn more about adoption in ancient Greece, especially as it is often asserted that adoption has been practiced since ancient Greek times as if a self-evident truth and as if adoption practices have remained largely unchanged since. For example, a 2008 commentary on Article 21 of the *United Nations Convention on the Rights of the Child* states, "Historically, adoption was used in Antiquity by the Greeks and Romans";[102] and the VLRC's 2016 consultation paper in relation to its *Review of the Adoption Act 1984* states, "Adoption was common in ancient Greece and ancient Rome ... Adoption records in ancient Greece date from the sixth century BCE."[103] Curiously, where such assertions are made in the context of advocating the continued use of adoption, the details of ancient Greek adoption practices tend to be mentioned only cursorily, if at all. This has made me wonder how much adoption proponents really know about the purposes, laws and practices of adoption in ancient Greek times and, further, how relevant those purposes, laws and practices may or may not be to the current context.

This chapter therefore explores the intentions and arrangements associated with adoption in ancient Athens,[104] the capital of ancient Greece, compared to contemporary adoption in my home state, Victoria. For this purpose, I read some key academic sources on the topic and tabularised the main messages below—I emphasise that I did not seek to employ a rigorous academic methodology or undertake a formal literature review.

---

101 Ibid.

102 Quoted from Sylvain Vité and Herve Boéchat, *A Commentary on the United Nations Convention on the Rights of the Child, Article 21: Adoption* (2008), p. 1.

103 Quoted from the Victorian Law Reform Commission's *Review of the Adoption Act 1984: Consultation Paper* (2016), p. 8.

104 For the purpose of simplicity, I have restricted consideration of adoption laws and practices in ancient Greece to those of ancient Athens. There is also documentation relating to the adoption practices of other significant places in ancient Greece, especially on the Greek islands of Crete and Rhodes, but the respective laws and practices were somewhat different to those of Athens.

Adoption in ancient Athens, Greece [Based on various academic sources[105]]	Adoption in contemporary Victoria, Australia [Based on the *Adoption Act 1984* (Vic), Adoption Regulations 2019, and the DJCS website]
Adoption was recognised as a legal institution in Athens but there was no attempt to encourage the practice of adoption, by law or otherwise.	Adoption is recognised as a legal institution in Victoria but the practice of adoption is not overtly encouraged. The Victorian Government has never overtly encouraged use of adoption specifically for children placed in out-of-home care who are unable to return to their parents' care. Instead, it introduced the Permanent Care Order (PCO) in 1992 for this purpose. However, amendments to the legislation made in 2014 prioritised adoption ahead of the PCO.[106] This change to the permanency hierarchy is incongruent with the Victorian Government's claim that it did/does not intend to increase adoptions from out-of-home care.[107]
The primary purpose of adoption was to prevent the extinction of a male lineage by providing a man with an heir.	Neither the purpose of adoption nor the object of the *Adoption Act 1984* is clearly stated in the Act. It is, however, implicit that the primary purpose of adoption is to provide for a child in need of ongoing parental care, and that the purpose of the *Adoption Act 1984* is to set out the circumstances, legal requirements and legal arrangements for adoption.

105 These sources are: Ilias Arnaoutoglou (1998) *Ancient Greek Laws: A Sourcebook*; Peter J. Conn (2013) *Adoption: A Brief Social and Cultural History*; Department of Economic and Social Affairs, Population Division (2009) *Child Adoption: Trends and Policies*; Sabine R. Huebner (2013) 'Adoption and Fosterage in the Ancient Eastern Mediterranean'; Hugh Lindsay (2009) *Adoption in the Roman World*; Hugh Lindsay (2010) 'Adoption and Heirship in Greece and Rome'; and Lene Rubinstein (1993) *Adoption in IV. Century Athens*.

106 The Permanent Care Order was specifically created through Victorian legislation in 1989 and implemented from 1992 in preference to adoption for the purpose of securing long-term family care (with kin or non-kin) for children unable to be reunified with their parents.

107 See Penny Mackieson (2019). Op. cit.

The interests of the adopter were paramount. Adoption was not concerned with the welfare of the adopted person, rather it was concerned to preserve the household—comprising a family's name and property.	The child's interests are paramount: "In the administration of this Act, the welfare and interests of the child concerned shall be regarded as the paramount consideration." (Section 9)
Adult male Athenian citizens of sound mind and free of duress could adopt, unless they: • already had a legitimate natural son (marriage between Athenian citizens was required for the creation of legitimate children), or • were adopted themselves and had not produced any legitimate natural male offspring for their adoptive family.	Eligibility to adopt is open to adults resident in Victoria, including: • couples who are married (for at least two years), • couples living in a recognised or registered domestic relationship (for at least two years), • single adults. An applicant may also be required to have Australian citizenship for eligibility to adopt a child from overseas.
Athenian citizenship was required for eligibility to be adopted. Mainly adult males were chosen for adoption, but also some boys and women. The choice of adoptee was entirely up to the adopter in the case of *inter vivos* and testamentary adoptions. The adopted person was usually, if not always, chosen from the adopter's close kin.	Eligibility to be adopted is open to: • children (i.e., aged under 18 years), whether or not they have previously been adopted, • adults who were raised by the respective adoptive applicant. Private adoption arrangements are prohibited—all adoptions, local and intercountry, must be arranged through an authorised adoption agency (except for adult adoptions). Adoption of a child by a relative of the child is discouraged, but exceptions can be made in particular circumstances where it is deemed to be in the child's best interests.

Foundlings of unknown parentage were raised as either slaves or foster children (fosterage), but were not formally adopted. Fosterage was primarily concerned with the child's welfare—it provided orphaned or abandoned children with a new home. Fosterage did not involve any legal change in the child's status or filiation.	Children can be placed in temporary foster care with kin or non-kin carers through either a voluntary arrangement or a court order. Foster/kinship care is considered temporary alternative family care for children unable to live with their natural parents.[108] Foster/kinship care does not involve any legal change in the child's status or filiation.
Adoption legally terminated the kinship ties between the adopted person and their natural father and paternal relatives. Adoption usually entailed the adoptee changing his name by dropping his natural father's name and taking on his adoptive father's name, as if born to his adoptive father. The adopted son could return to his natural father's family, but only if he first produced legitimate natural sons in his adoptive father's family.	Adoption legally terminates the kinship ties between the adopted person and their natural parents and paternal and maternal relatives. Adoption entails changing the original birth registration and legal name of the adoptee to the name of their adoptive parent(s), as if born to the adoptive parent(s).
If a son was born into the family after an adoption was completed, the adopted son and the natural son were entitled to equal shares of the inheritance.	An adopted person is entitled to a share of the inheritance equal to any child born into the family.
There were three different kinds of adoption: 1. While the adopter was alive (*inter vivos*), 2. By testament after the adopter's death (i.e. bequeathed in the deceased person's will), 3. Posthumously by a relative in the name of the deceased family member.	Only one type of adoption, known as 'full adoption' or 'plenary adoption',[109] is legally recognised in Victoria.

108 See Families, Fairness and Housing (2022) 'Families and Children: Foster Care'.

109 See Kerry O'Halloran (2021) *The Politics of Adoption: International Perspectives on Law, Policy and Practice* (Fourth Edition).

Adoption *inter vivos* involved a voluntary contract (oral and written) entered into by the two adults party to the adoption (adopter and adoptee) that was a complete and valid legal act ('full adoption'). The adopted son acquired the same rights and obligations as a legitimate natural son. This meant he would: • inherit his adoptive father's property, and • be obliged to care for his adoptive father in his old age, provide him with a proper burial when he died, and perform the customary funeral rights. The adopted son had immediate and uncontested rights to his inheritance upon his adoptive father's death, placing him in as strong a position as a legitimate natural son (unlike in testamentary adoption or posthumous adoption).	Intending adoptive parent(s) apply to the County Court of Victoria for ratification of the full/plenary adoption of the child. The child is the subject of the Adoption Order, rather than a legal party to it, although the child's wishes are considered as far as practicable. The adopted child acquires the same rights as any child born into the family.
If an adoptive father had a natural daughter, he usually married her to his adopted son to continue his family line through her children. This also ensured financial stability for the adoptive father's dependents. The incest taboo was not considered a problem in cases where the adopted son theoretically became his sister's husband.	The adopted person is treated as if born to the adoptive parent(s), therefore, marriage to an adoptive sibling or other close adoptive relative is prohibited. In regard to general laws relating to sexual offences, an adopted person is prohibited from knowingly marrying a sibling or other close relative within their natural family.

Testamentary adoption involved a legal act—the Will had to be ratified after the adopter's death by an inheritance procedure which involved adjudication by the people's court. Testamentary adoptions were often disputed by members of the adopter's family during the inheritance procedure. Testamentary adoption was probably more common than adoption *inter vivos* because, if the bequeather (adopter) had a legitimate natural son shortly before he died, that son automatically became his heir.	Not applicable.
Posthumous adoption involved a legal act requiring ratification by the people's court. In this case, the choice of the adoptee was made for the deceased adopter by one of the adopter's heirs. The adoptee was usually the heir by the rules of intestate succession (i.e. in the circumstance where the deceased had not made a will before he died). It was often a posthumously born grandson (the son of an adopter's legitimate natural daughter) who was adopted, even when the deceased adopter had never indicated intent to adopt his grandson. Posthumous adoption was probably more common than adoption *inter vivos*, and was also more difficult to regulate.	Not applicable.
Adoption and renunciation of adoption was held in public.	The granting or discharge of an Adoption Order is held in either a closed hearing of the County Court, or in chambers without a hearing.

Some similarities, but also numerous significant differences, between ancient Athenian adoption practices and contemporary Victorian adoption practices are evident in the table above.

In summary, adoption was important in ancient Athens to people of wealth—in particular, to men of wealth.[110] This is because ancient Athenian culture was both patriarchal and patrilineal. The head of the family was male; only men could legally own property; where the head of the family had no legitimate natural male heir he could choose to adopt; and thus there was a strong preference to adopt adult males from within the adopter's own kinship circle.[111] In contrast, adoption in Victoria has always predominantly involved children, both female and male. Adoption in ancient Athens was an inheritance system that developed to deal with situations of no legitimate natural male heir and thus was "quite complicated" and not without controversy.[112] It is unknown whether Athenians of lesser financial means practiced adoption in the same ways as rich Athenians,[113] as there are no records to indicate that adoptions occurred at all among the less wealthy and poor.[114] This has parallels with the contemporary practice of adoption and foster care in Victoria, in that adoptive applicants must be assessed as having adequate financial means and wealthier people tend to seek to adopt rather than become foster carers. Similarly, adoption was not officially encouraged in ancient Athens, nor is it officially encouraged in contemporary Victoria.

Adoption was developed for a specific purpose in ancient Athens—to address the interests of wealthy male citizens by providing a male heir where they had no legitimate natural son. Meanwhile, fosterage (which did not lead to formal adoption) was the preferred option for raising orphaned or abandoned children in ancient Athens. Therefore, foster care was viewed as a long-term option for caring for children. In contrast, in contemporary

---

110 See Hugh Lindsay (2009). Op. cit., p. 35.
111 See Hugh Lindsay (2010). Op. cit.
112 Ibid, p. 347.
113 See Lene Rubinstein (1993). Op. cit.
114 See Hugh Lindsay (2009). Op. cit.

Victoria, foster care is viewed as a temporary option for children in need of ongoing care by an alternative family. While the primary purpose of adoption is purportedly to address the welfare of such children, adoption is only one of a range of options available for this purpose and is not (overtly, at least) the preferred option for children in out-of-home care unable to be reunified with their parents. On the other hand, the Victorian Government made legislative changes in 2014 which preference adoption from out-of-home care ahead of the purpose-created Permanent Care Order (PCO). This is consistent with an unstated intent to increase the number of adoptions from out-of-home care.[115] In 2015, the Victorian Government made further legislative changes which expanded eligibility to adopt to include same-sex couples. This change is also consistent with an unstated intent to increase the number of child adoptions and, further, reflects a continuing preoccupation with ensuring intending parents' interests over the rights of vulnerable children and their natural parents—as was inherent in past forced adoption practices in Victoria.

Legal change to the status and identity of the adopted person, as if they were born to their adoptive parent(s), is inherent in both ancient Athenian and contemporary Victorian adoption. However, contemporary Victorian adoption is arguably more extreme. First, because it legally terminates the adopted person's kinship ties with both the maternal and paternal sides of their natural family, instead of only with the paternal side as in ancient Athenian adoption. Second, because contemporary Victorian adoption is predominantly arranged on behalf of the subject child, rather than as an equal party with the person (adult) to be adopted, as was

---

115 This argument is elaborated on pages 165–166 of my PhD thesis. The AIHW has also attributed the significant increase in known child adoptions by carers in Australia to the legislative changes made by the NSW Government to its permanency hierarchy, which preferences adoption immediately after reunification with parents (*Adoptions Australia 2019–20*, Op. cit., p. 39; and *Adoptions Australia 2020–21*, Op. cit., p. 26).

the case in ancient Athens in adoption *inter vivos*—the equivalent to full/plenary adoption now. In contemporary Victoria, adoption is purportedly undertaken in the best interests of the child. But even aside from any consideration of the child's human rights, it is difficult to justify the need for such draconian termination of the child's legal connections to their natural kin, given this feature of adoption was explicitly developed in ancient Greek times to serve the interests of the adopter. Furthermore, the ready availability of consumer genetic genealogy testing in the contemporary context illuminates the absurdity of continuing to legally create fictitious kin relationships through adoption.

It is evident that adoption has always been complicated. The adoption laws and practices developed millennia ago in ancient Athens were complex, even though designed for a clear and specific purpose—to serve the interests of adopters in regard to inheritance. Likewise, Victoria's *Adoption Act 1984* comprises a sizeable[116] and complicated set of laws and remains Victoria's primary adoption legislation, despite lacking clarity regarding its purpose and goals.[117] It is thus unsurprising that the Victorian Government's recent rhetoric in regard to developments concerning adoption is replete with mixed messages. For example, "to remove discrimination against the children of same-sex couples" but also "enhance the rights of LGBTI couples;"[118] "to design and establish Australia's first redress scheme for people affected by forced adoption" but apparently restricted to "Victorian women who had their children taken from them under heartbreaking historic forced adoption practices,"[119] curiously excluding the adopted people who were forcibly separated as babies from their mothers in the context

---

116 The *Adoption Act 1984* (Authorised Version No. 073) is 183 pages long.
117 See the Victorian Law Reform Commission's report (2017). Op. cit., pp. 24–27.
118 Quoted from Daniel Andrews (23 February 2015) 'Same-Sex Adoption A Step Closer With Review Of Laws'.
119 Quoted from Daniel Andrews and Jaclyn Symes (10 March 2022). Op. cit.

of the very same practices; and "to give [adult] adoptees the choice to include both their birth and adoptive parents on their birth certificates,"[120] while ignoring continuing calls to preserve an adopted individual's original or natural identity in the first place. The recent amendments to Victoria's adoption legislation are promoted by the Victorian Government as progressive social policy, but I would argue that they are actually regressive. I don't see how policy can be considered progressive if it intentionally elevates the interests of one group above the rights of another, or if it serves to covertly appropriate an institution that has long out-lived its original purpose for other contentious purposes.

Some adoption proponents maintain that introducing 'simple adoption'—which unfortunately sounds antithetically superficial and simplistic, given the complexities inherent in raising children born to other people—will fix the legacy of secrecy that remains foundational to contemporary adoption through the falsification of the adoptee's birth certificate.[121] In fact, last century, 'open adoption' was advocated for much the same purpose and resulted in the introduction of Victoria's *Adoption Act 1984*, yet problems have continued to be raised with the new open adoptions. Meanwhile, progressively fewer adoptions have been arranged in Victoria, and many times more PCOs than adoption orders have been granted since PCOs were implemented in 1992 (as shown in Figure 1 in Chapter 5). This would suggest that Victoria does not need another legal order to secure long-term alternative care placements for children in out-of-home care who need them—the fundamental problem with Victoria's child protection and out-of-home care system is not a lack of appropriate legal options.

---

120 Quoted from Jaclyn Symes (5 April 2022) 'Helping Adopted Victorians Record Their Birth History'.
121 See Karleen Gribble and Stacy Blythe (28 November 2019) 'Adoption Law Should Be Reformed to Give Children Legal Connections to Both of Their Families'; and Stacy Blythe and Karleen Gribble (2019) *Belonging in Two Families: Exploring Permanency Options for Children in Long-term Out-of-Home Care in Australia*.

There is a problem, however, with the continuing preoccupation of some well-meaning people in positions of influence to ensure the self-interests of intending and adoptive parents. For example, leading the recent campaign to introduce simple adoption in all Australian states and territories, including Victoria,[122] are NSW academics who are themselves foster and adoptive parents.[123] This apparent conflict of interest may explain the curious and controversial inclusion of a section on simple adoption that references their work in *Adoptions Australia 2019–20*.[124] The AIHW's annual report on adoptions in Australia had previously (since 1990–91) reported only on data and trends in relation to orders that have been granted, not legal options that have not been introduced and may never be. The use of the *Adoptions Australia* report as a platform to advocate for a new permanency option appears to have been unprecedented and presumably drew criticism, because there was no mention of simple adoption in the following year's *Adoptions Australia* report (for 2020–21).

In conclusion, the institution of adoption has been complicated from the time it was developed in ancient Greece specifically to serve the interests of adopters concerning disposal of their wealth. In contrast, adoption in contemporary Victoria purports to hold the welfare and interests of the child as paramount. Nevertheless, adoption law in contemporary Victoria is also complicated, and the primary purpose of adoption in the current context is far from clear. Whether or not the ongoing lack of clarity is intentional, adoption continues to be *done to* children; children are not treated

---

122 See Karleen Gribble's submission to the Victorian Law Reform Commission's Review of the Adoption Act 1984 (2016).

123 Dr Stacy Blythe is an experienced foster parent (see Dr Blythe's blurb on the International Foster Care Organisation's website) and Dr Karleen Gribble is an adoptive parent (see the Contents page in Tanya Bretherton, Karleen Gribble and Stacy Blythe's (2017) *Barriers to Adoption in Australia*).

124 See the Australian Institute of Health and Welfare's *Adoptions Australia 2019–20* report (2021), p. 4.

as equal rights-bearing parties to an Adoption Order, even when they become adults; and for 30 years Victoria has had a frequently-used purpose-specific PCO to secure ongoing alternative family care for children in out-of-home care who cannot be raised by their parents. Despite concerted efforts by NSW adoption advocates, adoption-from-care is not a policy that has been embraced in Victoria. This suggests that the institution of adoption not only has no clear purpose in contemporary Victoria but arguably has no clear relevance either.

Reflections

My deep concern regarding adoption in contemporary Victorian and wider Australian society has always been based on the draconian and unnecessary violation of natural identity and family connection rights involved. This concern remains unchanged from 2015 when my previous book, *Adoption Deception*, was published. As outlined in the next chapter, adoption policy and practice in Victoria also remains unchanged, despite much activity associated with several relevant inquiries conducted during the intervening period. The only significant change specifically intended to assist people adopted in Victoria—the option of an integrated birth certificate on attaining 18 years—was promised by the Victorian Government in March 2022 but is yet to be implemented.

Australian governments, including 'socially progressive' ones, seem to find dealing with past coercive and closed adoption practices—especially genuinely committing to not repeating them—unwanted as well as complex and controversial. This is evidenced, for example, through the hypocrisy of their deliberate facilitation of third-party medically assisted reproduction services which replicate some of the most harmful aspects of past forced adoption practices—such as allowing deliberately conceived children to be raised without ensuring they are informed of their origins and the identity of their natural parent(s). Clearly not all progress is actually an improvement.

Unfortunately, activity associated with addressing the aftermath of past adoption practices and debate on adoption-from-care policy seems to have served as an opportune distraction while morally problematic sperm donation and surrogacy practices have become embedded as key spokes in the relentless wheel of the market in babies. There is a thriving unregulated donor sperm market in Australia,[125] despite the fact that anonymous gamete donation is banned in every state and territory. Likewise, surrogacy—a process that intentionally removes a child from their natural parent(s)—is a growth area for Australia's Assisted Reproductive Technologies (ART) and legal industries,[126] despite the fact that commercial surrogacy is banned in every state and territory. Indeed, recent campaigning to change laws concerning ART services across Australian jurisdictions to increase 'reimbursement' for surrogate mothers seems to be aimed at erasing the distinction between 'altruistic' and 'commercial' surrogacy practices in favour of commercial surrogacy. Meanwhile, TV shows seem intent on normalising use of surrogacy.[127] A significant indication that surrogacy is now not only increasingly popular in this country but also increasingly supported by people in positions of influence is the recent awarding of a Medal of the Order of Australia to Sarah Jefford, a self-described 'family creation lawyer', for "services to the

---

125 See, for example, Tory Shepherd's article, "'I Had Two Babies Born Last Week": The Unregulated World of Australia's Online Sperm Donors' (6 February 2023).
126 See, for example, Hannah Walsh and Tegan Philpott's article, 'Surrogacy Is on the Increase in Australia, But Agreements Can Be Legally, Medically and Emotionally Complex' (18 December 2022).
127 For example, see 'The Surrogates' on *SBS* One; or read Laura Jackel's article, 'Everything We Know About the New Fertility TV Series Big Miracles' (3 February 2023).

law, her work with the surrogacy community and for leading the change for surrogacy in Australia."[128]

The clear disconnect between past forced adoption practices and third-party ART procedures is wilful. As I argued in my speech at VANISH's 2022 AGM,[129] Australian governments' persistent lack of focus on the rights of children continues to passively, but effectively, elevate the interests of intending parents in adoption and third-party reproduction policy, law and practice. More than that, Australian governments also actively promote the interests of intending parents over the rights of children through supporting the medicalisation of infertility, and broadening eligibility for access to third-party medically assisted reproduction services and adoption programs. From my perspective, this is a blueprint for the commodification of children, creating expectations for increased supply.

Governments of all political persuasions have always liked to be seen as supportive of growing families and caring for children in need. Nowadays, apparently, the more 'diverse' the families the better, irrespective of the ethical issues associated with family formation/reproduction methods used by people who are infertile for social reasons. Indeed, people generally continue to appear more interested in 'happily-ever-after' and 'forever family' narratives in family and ART policy-making than concerned about unanticipated consequences or known negative outcomes, particularly in relation to the children. This probably explains why Australia's major political parties also continue to hold a place for adoption, though for different reasons: the right-leaning because they favour adoption as a practical 'solution' to the nation's ongoing

---

128 See Sarah Jefford's blog, 'Sarah Jefford Awarded Medal of the Order of Australia' (2023).
129 Refer to Appendix V: Speech at VANISH AGM, November 2022.

child protection crisis,[130] and the left-leaning because they favour adoption as a legal means to normalise non-heteronormative families.[131]

Indeed, now it is apparently also widely held that identity is a purely social construct that an individual, including a child, can choose subject to personal preference, independent of hereditary facts. Ergo the legislative changes made in 2019 enabling children born in Victoria to change the sex descriptor on their birth certificate to match their preferred gender. Even if such thinking were reasonable,[132] it is neither logical nor fair that the natural identity and name of a child adopted in Victoria is legally cancelled and replaced with fictitious kin relationships years before they are in a position to make an informed choice about their preferred identity and the ramifications for their descendants. It is unreasonable and unfair, if not also absurd in this day and age, that an adopted child is denied the opportunity to *retain* their natural pre-adoptive identity. Furthermore, when the adopted individual does eventually attain the capacity to understand the importance of their pre-adoptive identity and reasonably chooses to reclaim it, as illustrated by my case, the process involved for someone adopted in Victoria to 'opt out' of their adoption and reclaim their original identity is unreasonably complex, unfair and discriminatory.

Despite progressive rhetoric regarding individual choice in relation to identity and inclusiveness in relation to family formation methods, current policy, law and practice in these areas is both deceptive and regressive in terms of the rights of the child and this

---

130 For example, see Christian Porter's article, 'Adoption and Child Protection' (29 October 2014).

131 For example, see Farah Tomazin's article, 'Same-Sex Couples a Step Closer to Equal Adoption Rights in Victoria' (21 February 2015).

132 The reasonableness of such thinking is increasingly challenged, with growing concern and pushback in relation to the "gender affirmative care" model that underpins treatment in Australia's health systems for children who experience gender dysphoria. For example, see Claire Lehmann's article, 'Acceptance, Not Surgery, Solution To Teen Trans Anxiety' (10 February 2023).

carries through into their adulthood. The cycle of problematic and poor practices that fuels the market in babies thus seems never-ending. This deeply saddens and disappoints me and has often also made me feel like a solitary goldfish swimming against an open-ocean current, despite being engaged with many substantive lifebuoys. Whether or not people in general care, I know that my concerns are shared domestically and abroad by many. For example, those involved in the communities of VANISH Inc.,[133] Donor Conceived Australia,[134] and the International Coalition for the Abolition of Surrogate Motherhood,[135] of which several activist-authors have been published by Spinifex Press.[136] Notwithstanding, I have found advocating for the rights of children in the context of adoption, donor conception and surrogacy to be infuriating and exhausting.

Thankfully, my anger has dissipated greatly with the improvements in relation to my own identity—especially since my de-adoption and subsequent decision to focus on establishing meaningful social connections with my natural family members in Greece. For this purpose, I've resumed learning the Greek language and am planning my second trip to Greece in April–May 2023 to further immerse myself in Greek culture, as well as to meet my siblings and, hopefully also, my mother. My friend, Gonda Van Steen, has helpfully encapsulated my mission in the first chapter of a new book that shares stories from among the several thousand

---

133 See VANISH Inc.'s website.
134 See Donor Conceived Australia's Facebook page.
135 See the website of the Coalition Internationale pour l'Abolition de la Maternité de Substitution (CIAMS).
136 For example, Kajsa Ekis Ekman (2013) *Being and Being Bought: Prostitution, Surrogacy and the Split Self*; Renate Klein (2017) *Surrogacy: A Human Rights Violation*; Jennifer Lahl, Melinda Tankard Reist and Renate Klein (Eds) (2019) *Broken Bonds: Surrogate Mothers Speak Out*; and Marie-Josèphe Devillers and Ana-Luana Stoicea-Deram (Eds) (2021) *Towards the Abolition of Surrogate Motherhood*.

Greek-American adoptees who comprised the first significant wave of intercountry adoption after the Second World War:[137]

> Many of them have fully committed to searching for their roots, which is a quest for truth and recognition as much as for blood-related family and a deeper sense of belonging.

All I've ever wanted is the deep sense of belonging associated with knowing and being connected with who and where I've come from. Now I know that my heritage is Greek, actually. I'm proud of my Greek heritage and that it is now formally recognised, too. That is what my identity means to me. Truth be told, it's probably what identity means to most people, though they may not articulate it as such unless their own identity has been undermined. I've worked hard to legally reclaim and integrate my natural identity. I don't believe this is because my perspective on identity is extreme but rather because adoption is extreme. I've deliberately chosen to no longer be a victim of the extreme historically-contorted socio-legal institution of adoption.

I've also deliberately chosen to share my story here in the hope that others in a similar situation will be encouraged. What better way for an adopted person to express that they no longer accept the numerous ways in which their identity challenges are gaslighted, their identity needs disrespected and their identity rights ignored than choosing to become de-adopted. What better way to illustrate the long overdue need for major change in relation to adoption policy, legislation and practice than through a flood of court applications by adopted people to discharge their respective adoptions. Bring on the flood! Φέρτε την πλημμύρα!

---

137 See Gonda Van Steen's 'Adoption's Unfinished Business' in Mary Cardaras (Ed.) *Voices of the Lost Children of Greece: Oral Histories of Cold War International Adoption* (2023), p. 14.

CHAPTER 5

Chronology since 2015

Since publication of *Adoption Deception* in 2015, the annual number of adoptions in Australia overall has fluctuated somewhat, although the relatively small number of adoptions in the state of Victoria has continued a gradually downward trend. This is depicted in Table 1 below, which shows that in recent years, there have been roughly 300 adoptions per year in Australia and roughly 20 adoptions per year in Victoria. It has been estimated that approximately 64,000 Victorians have been adopted since 1928 when the first adoption legislation (the *Adoption of Children Act 1928*) was introduced in the state,[138] and that more than 45,000 children were adopted in Victoria during the 30-year period from 1945 to 1975.[139] The statistics presented in Table 1 thus serve to reinforce that the vast majority of people impacted by adoptions in Victoria are those impacted by past adoptions, like mine, rather than by adoptions finalised since implementation of the *Adoption Act 1984*.[140]

---

138 See Justice and Community Safety (2022) 'Adopt a Child' Melbourne: Victoria State Government.

139 See Christin Quirk (2013). Op. cit.

140 See VANISH Inc's submission to the Victorian Law Reform Commission's Review of the Adoption Act 1984 (2016), pp. 17–18.

Table 1: Annual totals of finalised adoptions in Australia (by Australian and Intercountry children), carer/known child adoptions (including in Victoria and NSW), and adoptions in Victoria, from 2014–15 to 2021–22.[141]

Year	2014 –15	2015 –16	2016 –17	2017 –18	2018 –19	2019 –20	2020 –21	2021 -22
Finalised adoptions in Australia								
Total adoptions	292	278	315	330	310	334	264	208
Australian children	209	196	246	265	253	297	222	192
Intercountry children	83	82	69	65	57	37	42	16
Carer/Known child adoptions								
Australia	152	151	204	233	211	249	183	161
Victoria	5	10	1	3	3	3	1	0
NSW	108	97	152	186	165	201	122	122
Adoptions in Victoria								
Total adoptions	38	34	23	22	20	21	18	8
Carer/Known child	5	10	1	3	3	3	1	0
Local	24	15	14	12	12	14	14	8
Intercountry	9	9	8	7	5	4	3	0

The significant decrease over time in the use of Adoption Orders in Victoria is demonstrated in Figure 1 below, which also shows the increasing use of Permanent Care Orders (PCOs) for children unable to be safely raised by their parents since PCOs were implemented in 1992.

---

141 This data was sourced from the Australian Institute of Health and Welfare's annual *Adoptions Australia* reports for the respective years.

Figure 1: Numbers of PCOs and Adoption Orders granted in Victoria from 1992–93 to 2021–22.[142]

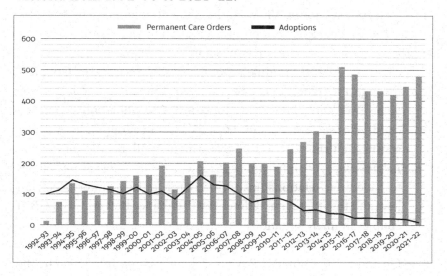

Key developments in my personal adoption journey since the publication of *Adoption Deception* in 2015 are summarised in chronological order below. These are juxtaposed with developments in the broader context of adoption policy, legislation and practice relating to Victoria and interstate that occurred during the same period.

August 2015

I commenced full-time PhD studies in Social Work at the University of Melbourne on the history and outcomes of permanent care in Victoria.

---

142 This data was sourced from the Australian Institute of Health and Welfare's annual *Adoptions Australia* and *Child Protection Australia* reports for the respective years. The number of Permanent Care Orders granted for 2021–22 was sourced from the 2021–22 Annual Report of the Children's Court of Victoria.

October 2015

06: The *Adoption Amendment (Adoption by Same-Sex Couples) Bill 2015* was introduced to the Victorian Parliament to amend the *Adoption Act 1984* to enable the adoption of children by same-sex couples.

06: The Victorian Government issued a media release:

- claiming "Adoption Equality for Children of Same-Sex Couples" through introduction of the *Adoption Amendment (Adoption by Same-Sex Couples) Bill 2015*, "to remove discrimination against the children of same-sex couples from Victorian adoption laws";[143]
- stating that the Victorian Government "will also introduce the *Relationships Amendment Bill 2015*, which will enable more couples to have their relationships formally recognised under Victorian law [and that these] amendments will enhance the rights of LGBTI couples in many situations";[144]
- attributing the Bill to "recommendations made by Eamonn Moran QC in his Adoption Act Review" which was commissioned by the Victorian Government "to consider the legal changes required to permit adoption of children by same-sex couples under Victorian law" and examined "how best to legislate for [this], not whether or not the change should happen."[145]

26: Richard Stubbs interviewed me about *Adoption Deception* on ABC 774 radio.

28: A launch event was held for *Adoption Deception* by VANISH Inc. in Carlton, Victoria.

28: VANISH's Committee of Management elected me to the position of Chairperson of VANISH Inc.

30: I delivered a paper on behalf of VANISH, 'How to Avoid Repeating Adoption Mistakes of Australia's Past', at the 5th Annual Sector Research Symposium in Melbourne.

---

143 Quoted from Martin Foley (6 October 2015) 'Adoption Equality For Children Of Same-Sex Couples'.

144 Ibid.

145 Quoted from Daniel Andrews (23 February 2015). Op. cit.

November 2015

28: A launch event was held for *Adoption Deception* at the Australian Association of Social Workers' (AASW) National Symposium in Sydney.

December 2015

15: The *Adoption Amendment (Adoption by Same-Sex Couples) Act 2015* received assent,[146] thereby amending Victoria's principal adoption legislation (*Adoption Act 1984*) to enable the adoption of children by same-sex couples.

16: Victoria's Attorney-General (A-G) asked the Victorian Law Reform Commission (VLRC) to provide recommendations to the Victorian Government on the modernisation of the *Adoption Act 1984* and the *Adoption Regulations 2008*.[147]

January 2016

10: I co-presented a session, 'Learnings from past adoption policies, practices and outcomes in Australia', with other VANISH representatives at The 5th International Conference on Adoption Research (ICAR5) in Auckland, New Zealand (NZ).

12: A lunchtime launch event was held for *Adoption Deception* at ICAR5 in Auckland, NZ.

14: I presented a paper, 'Children's rights and the neo-liberal politics of adoption in Australia', at the Redefining Family Conference in Auckland, NZ.

March 2016

The permanency amendments to the *Children, Youth and Families Act 2005* that were passed in September 2014 commenced operation in Victoria.

---

146 See Victorian Legislation (2015) Adoption Amendment (Adoption by Same-Sex Couples) Bill 2015.

147 See Victorian Law Reform Commission (2015) 'Adoption Act: Terms of Reference'.

July 2016

A critique of *Adoption Deception* by two NSW-based adoption proponents was published in an Australian child welfare journal.[148]

August 2016

10: The VLRC released a Consultation Paper as part of its *Review of the Adoption Act 1984*.[149]

18: The Victorian Government announced the introduction to Parliament of the *Births, Deaths and Marriages Bill 2016* to enable trans, gender diverse and intersex Victorians to amend their birth certificates.[150] The Bill was defeated.[151]

September 2016

01: As requested by the Victorian Minister for Families and Children, the Commission for Children and Young People (CCYP) commenced an inquiry into the outcomes of the first six months of operation of the permanency amendments to the *Children, Youth and Families Act 2005*.[152]

22: I delivered the keynote speech, 'Adoption: The Elephant in the Social Worker's Office', at the University of Melbourne Social Work Alumni Association Annual Dinner.

29: Beth Matthews interviewed me on the topic of adoption on her Radical Philosophy program on 3CR Community Radio.

October 2016

I received the results from an AncestryDNA test indicating I had 0% ethnicity from the UK and Ireland but 69% Greek ethnicity. I asked Ancestry to check whether my sample had been misidentified in their lab, and they confirmed there had been no mix-up.

---

148 See Susan Tregeagle and Deidre Cheers (2016). Op. cit.

149 See Jenny Mikakos (30 August 2016) 'Call to Comment on Outdated Adoption Laws'; and Victorian Law Reform Commission (2016) *Review of the Adoption Act 1984: Consultation Paper*.

150 See Martin Pakula and Martin Foley (18 August 2016) 'Birth Certificates to Reflect True Identity'.

151 See Victorian Legislation (2022) 'Births, Deaths and Marriages Registration Amendment Bill'.

152 See the Commission for Children and Young People (2017). Op. cit.

06: Beth Matthews interviewed me on the topic of permanent care on her Radical Philosophy program on 3CR Community Radio.

14: *The Times-Spectator* published a long letter that I authored on behalf of VANISH, titled 'Adoption laws should not sever biological ties', about the *Adoption Amendment (Adoption by Same-Sex Couples) Act 2015*.

20: *New Matilda* published (online) my article, 'Birth Certificates: The Elephant in the Room in Gender and Adoption Debates'.

November 2016

19: Rod Quinn interviewed me as Chair of VANISH on the topic of 'Adoption in Australia' on his Overnights program on ABC Radio.

December 2016

The Parliament of South Australia (SA) passed the *Adoption (Review) Amendment Act 2016*, which made significant changes to adoption laws in that state. These included broadening eligibility to adopt to include same-sex couples; removing adoption information vetoes; incorporating the Aboriginal and Torres Strait Islander Child Placement Principle into the Objects and Guiding Principles of the Act; providing a definition of parties to an adoption; enabling adults to be adopted; ensuring that an adopted child's first name is maintained, except in special circumstances; broadening the grounds for discharge of an Adoption Order; enabling parties to an adoption to be notified about the death of another party; and enabling people adopted in SA to have an integrated birth certificate.[153] Most of the changes were to be implemented progressively during 2017.[154]

February 2017

The VLRC's Report from its *Review of the Adoption Act 1984* was submitted to the Victorian Government.

---

153 See the Government of South Australia (2022) 'Change to the Adoption Act'.
154 See the Australian Institute of Health and Welfare's *Adoptions Australia 2016–17, Appendices A and B* (2017), p. 9.

June 2017

The CCYP submitted *Safe and Wanted*, the report from its inquiry into the early outcomes of the permanency amendments, to the Victorian Minister for Families and Children.

07: The VLRC's Report from its *Review of the Adoption Act 1984* was tabled in Parliament.[155] The Report made 88 recommendations of which the most significant was that "The *Adoption Act 1984* (Vic) should be repealed and replaced with a new Adoption Act" (#1).[156] It also recommended the introduction of optional integrated birth certificates for adopted people (#24 and #25).[157]

07: The Victorian Government released a statement welcoming the VLRC's Report from its *Review of the Adoption Act 1984* and promising it "will carefully consider the report and its recommendations, and start implementing changes to policies and service delivery to address some of the immediate issues raised."[158]

December 2017

11: My first academic article during the course of my PhD studies was published, titled 'Permanency Planning and Ideology in Western Child Welfare Systems: Implications for Victoria'.

11: A letter I submitted to the editor was published in response to the critique of *Adoption Deception* (published in July 2016 in the same child welfare journal), titled 'The Silencing of Lived Experience: The Author's Response to a Review of *Adoption Deception*'.

14: The Report from the CCYP's Inquiry into the early outcomes of the permanency amendments, *Safe and Wanted*,[159] was released to the public by the Minister for Families and Children. The Report made 40 recommendations, including "That the Victorian Government amends the CYFA 2005 to remove adoption from the hierarchy of permanency objectives, noting that this change will not affect the

---

155 See Victorian Law Reform Commission (2017). Op. cit.
156 Ibid, p. xxvii.
157 Ibid, p. xxxii.
158 Quoted from Jenny Mikakos and Martin Pakula (7 June 2017) 'Victorian Government Welcomes Adoption Review'.
159 See the Commission for Children and Young People (2017). Op. cit.

availability of adoption orders under the *Adoption Act 1984* where a child has been subject to child protection intervention and adoption is in their best interests" (#2).[160]

March 2018
14: My second academic article during the course of my PhD studies was published, titled 'Informing Permanent Care Discourses: A Thematic Analysis of Parliamentary Debates in Victoria'.

28: The Australian Parliament announced that the House of Representatives Standing Committee on Social Policy and Legal Affairs had "commenced an inquiry into local adoption, with a view to establishing whether there are any unnecessary barriers to adoptions in Australia."[161]

May 2018
14: I made a written submission to the National Inquiry into Local Adoption.[162]

July 2018
My third academic article during the course of my PhD studies was published, titled 'Increasing rigor and reducing bias in qualitative research: A document analysis of parliamentary debates using applied thematic analysis'.

October 2018
The Minister for Families and Children unveiled 'Taken Not Given', a sculpture commissioned as a memorial to those separated by adoption,[163] which was funded by the Victorian Government, in Melbourne.[164]

---

160 Ibid, p. 23.
161 Quoted from Parliament of Australia (28 March 2018) 'New review into barriers to local adoption'.
162 See Penny Mackieson (2018) 'Submission to the House of Representatives Standing Committee on Social Policy and Legal Affairs National Inquiry into Local Adoption' (Submission No. 61).
163 See Anne Ross (2019) 'Taken Not Given—of Love and Loss'.
164 See ARMS (28 October 2018) 'Unveiling of the Memorial Statue in Melbourne 26 October 2018'.

November 2018

The report of the House of Representatives Standing Committee on Social Policy and Legal Affairs from its inquiry into local adoption, *Breaking Barriers: A National Adoption Framework for Australian Children*,[165] was tabled in the Australian Parliament. The Report advocated 'open adoption' as a solution to children being "bounced" around the child protection and out-of-home care system "from one foster home to another" or who "experience significant trauma where their safety and welfare is at significant risk,"[166] and as a means of making adoption more viable and increasing the "very low" number of adoptions now occurring in Australia.[167] The Report made seven recommendations aimed at promoting adoptions across all Australian states and territories. The Report included a Dissenting Report by the Labor Party members of the Inquiry Committee.

December 2018

I received the results from a 23andMe DNA test. The results were consistent with those from my AncestryDNA test of 2016, indicating that I have 0% ethnicity from the UK and Ireland and predominantly Greek ethnicity.

January 2019

I submitted my PhD thesis, titled 'The Introduction and Implementation of Permanent Care Orders in Victoria', for examination.

February 2019

I resigned from the positions of Chairperson and Member of the Committee of Management of VANISH Inc. to focus on my own adoption-related issues.

---

165 See Parliament of Australia (2018) *Breaking Barriers: A National Adoption Framework for Australian Children*.
166 Ibid, p. vix.
167 Ibid, p. vix.

March 2019

Bruce Minahan (my partner) and Patrick Minahan (our son) took AncestryDNA tests. As expected, the results clearly indicated that I'm Patrick's mother, Bruce is Patrick's father, and Patrick is our son; that Bruce's ethnic ancestry originates predominantly from the UK and Ireland; and that Patrick's ethnic ancestry is approximately 37% Greek.

13: I lodged a second application with Monash Health under Freedom of Information (FOI) provisions seeking records relating to my birth and three-week period at the Queen Victoria Memorial Hospital (QVMH) in 1963 before my placement for adoption.[168]

16: I presented 'An Adoptee's Perspective on Surrogacy' at *Broken Bonds and Big Money: An International Conference on Surrogacy* held at RMIT University in Melbourne.

April 2019

01: I commenced employment as a Research Officer with Jesuit Social Services on a 3-month project (contracted from 1 April–30 June 2019).

05: I received a response from Monash Health to my second FOI application advising they were unable to locate medical records relating to me or my mother, reiterating that those records had presumably been destroyed.

13: I phoned Gwen,[169] my official natural mother, and asked her to take an AncestryDNA test to clarify our genetic relationship, to which she agreed.

May 2019

03: I phoned Gwen to request the results of her AncestryDNA test. The results confirmed we are not genetically related.

09: I lodged an application with the Victorian Government's Adoption Information Service (AIS)[170] to seek my *real* adoption records.

---

168 I made my first FOI application to Monash Health in 2014.
169 "Gwen" is an alias first name.
170 AIS was then known as FIND, the acronym for Family Information Networks and Discovery.

22: My fourth academic article from my PhD studies was published, titled 'Permanent Care Orders in Victoria: A Thematic Analysis of Implementation Issues'.

28: The Victorian Parliament's Legislative Assembly passed a motion referring "an inquiry into support services and responses to the issue of historical forced adoptions in Victoria to the Legal and Social Issues Committee for consideration and report no later than 31 December 2020."[171]

June 2019

13: AIS informed me they had found records identifying my real natural mother but were only able to provide non-identifying information, advising that I needed to apply to the County Court of Victoria for the release of identifying information. AIS agreed to outreach to my putative mother in Greece on my behalf.

18: The Victorian Government announced the passage of its *Births, Deaths and Marriages Registration Amendment* laws that were first introduced to Parliament in 2016. "The new laws will allow applicants to self-nominate the sex listed in their birth registration as male, female, or any other gender diverse or non-binary descriptor of their own choice. ... Children will also be able to apply to alter the sex recorded on their birth certificate, with parental support and a supporting statement from a doctor, registered psychologist or another prescribed confirming person that the decision is in the best interests of the child."[172] The Bill was passed by both houses of Parliament on 27 August 2019 and received assent on 3 September 2019.[173]

---

171 Quoted from the Legislative Assembly Legal and Social Issues Committee (2019) 'Terms of Reference: Inquiry into Responses to Historical Forced Adoptions in Victoria'.

172 Quoted from Jill Hennessy, Martin Foley and Jenny Mikakos (18 June 2019) 'Fairer Birth Certificates For Trans And Gender Diverse Victorians'.

173 See Victorian Legislation (2022) 'Births, Deaths and Marriages Registration Amendment Bill 2019'.

26: I was notified that the examiners of my PhD thesis recommended I be awarded the Degree of Doctor of Philosophy without further examination or amendment.

July 2019

01: Delivery of adoption services in Victoria transferred from the Department of Health and Human Services (DHHS) to the Department of Justice and Community Safety (DJCS). Adoption services include local adoption, intercountry adoption, information about past adoptions, and adoption relinquishment counselling.[174]

08: I commenced an ongoing Policy, Research and Advocacy Officer position with Jesuit Social Services.

31: AIS informed me they had phoned my putative mother in Greece using a Greek interpreter. They recommended I hold off applying to the County Court until they'd done as much as possible to confirm she is my mother.

AIS also informed me they had identified the adopted person whose identity they believed mine was swapped with at the QVMH.

August 2019

06: I commenced my first term of a CAE beginner's Greek language course.

23: I attended a conference, DNA Down Under, in Melbourne and met the Senior Director, International Programming with Ancestry. I disclosed the discovery of my Greek ethnicity through an AncestryDNA test and how it had led to the further discovery that I was misidentified prior to my adoption. He provided contact details for the producer of Artemis Films which makes the series *Every Family Has A Secret* (EFHAS) for SBS.

September 2019

The Australian Government released its *Response to the House of Representatives Standing Committee on Social Policy and Legal Affairs report: Breaking Barriers: A National Adoption Framework*

---

174 See Families, Fairness and Housing (2022) 'Adoption Victoria'; and Justice and Community Safety (2022) 'Adoption'.

for Australian Children. The response emphasised that the "State and territory governments are responsible for administering legislation in relation to the adoption of Australian children" and recognised that some of them "support adoption as a viable option for children in out-of-home care more strongly than others do."[175]

October 2019

01: AIS informed me of the first name given to me by my putative Greek mother when I was born, but not her family name (because that would have identified her).

15: I commenced my second term of the CAE beginner's Greek language course.

22: AIS informed me that their letter to my putative mother had been translated into Greek and sent to Greece.

November 2019

06: Victoria's Legislative Assembly Legal and Social Issues Standing Committee launched its Inquiry into Responses to Historical Forced Adoptions in Victoria.[176]

29: Bruce and I met with AIS to discuss my application to the County Court for release of identifying information about my putative mother in Greece.

December 2019

01: I lodged an Application for Release of Information under s.99(1) or s.100(1) of the *Adoption Act 1984* with the County Court of Victoria for all relevant records and information pertaining to the correct identity of my natural mother.

17: My PhD was conferred at a graduation ceremony for the University of Melbourne's Faculty of Medicine, Dentistry and Health Sciences.

175 See Parliament of Australia (2019) *Government Response: Breaking Barriers: A National Adoption Framework for Australian Children*, p. 2.

176 See Legislative Assembly Legal and Social Issues Standing Committee (6 November 2019) 'Forced Adoptions Inquiry Launched'.

January 2020

23: AIS informed me that their report in relation to my Application for Release of Information had been delivered to the County Court that day.

February 2020

02: I sent a confidential written submission to the Parliamentary Inquiry into Historical Responses to Forced Adoptions in Victoria.

15: I chartered a yacht cruise around the Small Cyclades in the Aegean Sea for October 2020 through a sailing company in Greece.

March 2020

04: I confirmed the dates for our chartered yacht cruise around the Small Cyclades.

07: I asked Flight Centre to book flights and accommodation for me, Bruce and Patrick for a trip to Greece in September-October 2020 and to organise travel insurance to cover any COVID-19-related issues.

11: I received the itinerary from Flight Centre for our planned trip to Greece and the invoice for payment.

14: I advised Flight Centre we had decided to postpone our trip to Greece due to the rapid escalation of concerns and restrictions relating to COVID-19 in Australia during the previous two days, including the Australian Government's recommendation against any unnecessary travel.

16: I advised the sailing company in Greece of our decision to postpone our cruise due to the rapid escalation of developments in Australia in relation to managing the COVID-19 crisis.

25: AIS informed me of the results of forensic DNA tests taken by Gwen and the person whose identity they believed mine was swapped with, which confirmed that their genetic relationship is mother-daughter.

31: The Victorian Government introduced Stage 3 COVID-19 restrictions across the state (Lockdown 1 commenced).[177]

---

177 The dates for the imposition and lifting of each of the six COVID-19 related lockdowns in Victoria were sourced from The Big Australia Bucket List (2022) 'Timeline of Every Victoria Lockdown (Dates and Restrictions)'.

April 2020

06: I received a letter from the County Court informing me they had communicated with my "potential birth mother" and the person I was "potentially switched with at birth" seeking their consent by 30 June 2020 to the release of identifying information.

11: I contacted Professor Gonda Van Steen,[178] author of *Adoption, Memory, and Cold War Greece: Kid pro quo?* (2019) about the post-war adoptions of more than 3,000 Greek children into the United States.

May 2020

01: Subsequent to the *Births, Deaths and Marriages Registration Amendment Act 2019*, the Victorian Government announced implementation of the changes enabling trans and gender diverse people born in Victoria to choose the sex descriptor recorded on their birth certificate through an administrative process administered by Births, Deaths and Marriages (BDM).[179]

12: The Victorian Government lifted the Stage 3 COVID-19 restrictions across the state (Lockdown 1 ended).

June 2020

10: AIS informed me they'd had a long phone conversation with my mother in Greece to explain the reason for the correspondence to her from the County Court of Victoria.

July 2020

09: The Victorian Government re-imposed Stage 3, and then introduced Stage 4, COVID-19 restrictions across the state (Lockdown 2 commenced).

14: Her Honour Judge Davis of the County Court of Victoria ordered that the Secretary, DJCS, release to me information relating to Donna,[180] the adopted person whose identity mine was swapped with at the QVMH.

---

178 Professor Van Steen's profile is available on King's College London's website.
179 See Jill Hennessy and Martin Foley (1 May 2020) 'Laws Commence To Deliver Fairer Birth Certificates'.
180 "Donna" is an alias first name.

22: I met (remotely) with AIS to clarify the documents and process for release, as ordered by Her Honour; to learn key identifying details; and to discuss possible next steps to correct my birth records given the limitations of the relevant legislation and BDM procedures.

23: The *Births, Deaths and Marriages Registration Amendment Bill 2020* was introduced to the Parliament of the Australian Capital Territory (ACT), proposing changes to make it easier for young transgender, intersex and gender diverse people to change their given names and sex details on their birth certificate, and to provide for integrated birth certificates for adopted persons.[181]

24: The relevant identifying records were released to me by AIS in accordance with the County Court order of 14 July 2020. The records indicate I was born to Georgia,[182] who was single at the time and whose family name was Zagarelou; and who registered my birth with her family name and her mother's first name. There was no information identifying my father.

August 2020

13: AIS informed me they'd made a phone call to Georgia the previous day to explain the outcome of my County Court application. The conversation was brief because Georgia indicated she did not wish to be contacted by AIS ever again or accept any contact from me.

13: AIS informed me it had been decided they would not attempt any further outreach to Georgia; they would not seek relevant QVMH medical records from Monash Health; and they would close my case now that Donna's adoption records had been released to me. However, they would continue to pursue legal advice in regard to correcting my birth records.

24: I wrote to Victoria's A-G seeking clarification regarding the scope of AIS's responsibilities in relation to helping remediate my situation.

28: I had my first session with a private counsellor in relation to my adoption and identity situation.

---

181 See The Greens ACT (23 July 2020) 'Recognising the Lived Experience of Canberrans in Birth Documents'.

182 "Georgia" is an alias first name.

September 2020

09: AIS informed me that they'd received my letter to the A-G and that I would receive a formal response in due course. AIS expressed that we seemed to have had a miscommunication; that my case remained open; that they would outreach to my brothers in Greece on my behalf; and that the legal advice they were seeking would probably now be expedited to inform the Ministerial response to my letter.

11: I had my second session with the private counsellor.

25: I had my third session with the private counsellor.

28: The NSW Parliament passed the *Adoption Legislation Amendment (Integrated Birth Certificates) Bill 2020* and it subsequently received assent. This legislation amended the *Adoption Act 2000* (NSW) and the *Births, Deaths and Marriages Registration Act 1995* (NSW) to enable adopted persons to access an integrated birth certificate.[183]

October 2020

15: AIS updated me on their unsuccessful outreaches to my brothers in Greece. AIS also advised that no other female babies were born to Greek mothers at the QVMH on or around the date of my birth.

19: I contacted the producer of EFHAS who was very interested in my story and felt EFHAS could tell it.

28: The Victorian Government lifted the Stage 3/Stage 4 COVID-19 restrictions across the state (Lockdown 2 ended).

30: I had my fourth session with the private counsellor.

November 2020

13: I had my fifth session with the private counsellor.

14: AIS updated me on their still unsuccessful outreaches to my brothers in Greece and informed me that they'd written to Monash Health requesting QVMH records for me and my mother, but none had been found.

15: I discussed with AIS BDM's limited capacity to correct my original birth record. BDM could remove Gwen's details; however, my official

---

183 See Parliament of New South Wales (2022) 'Adoption Legislation Amendment (Integrated Birth Certificates) Bill 2020'.

'original' name would have to remain the name Gwen gave her baby, unless another application was made to the County Court.

16: In accordance with the legislative changes made through the *Adoption Legislation Amendment (Integrated Birth Certificates) Act 2020*, integrated birth certificates were implemented in NSW, to be issued routinely for all persons subsequently adopted in NSW and available on application to people adopted in NSW prior to November 2020.[184]

19: I specifically requested written advice from DJCS regarding the legal status of my adoption, given I was misidentified at the time of my adoption.

December 2020

07: I gave oral evidence at a Public Hearing of the Parliamentary Inquiry into Responses to Historical Forced Adoption in Victoria.[185]

08: AIS informed me about a recent phone call they'd had with Georgia made in the context of an attempt to contact Nikos,[186] Georgia's son.

10: My article titled 'Adoption, Deception, and DNA Questions', was published as a Member Contribution in the December 2020 edition of *Voice*, the regular newsletter of VANISH Inc.[187]

11: I had my sixth session with the private counsellor.

January 2021

19: AIS released to me a copy of the letter they received from Monash Health regarding my QVMH records, but advised it would be a few more weeks before they could provide their legal advice regarding the status of my adoption because the DJCS Legal Unit was very short staffed.

February 2021

13: The Victorian Government imposed snap Stage 4 COVID-19 restrictions across the state (Lockdown 3 commenced).

---

184 See Communities and Justice (2022) 'Introducing Integrated Birth Certificates'.
185 See Parliament of Victoria (2021) 'Hearings and Transcripts, Inquiry into Responses to Historical Forced Adoptions in Victoria'.
186 "Nikos" is an alias first name.
187 See VANISH Inc. (2022) 'About VANISH'.

17: The Victorian Government lifted the Stage 4 COVID-19 restrictions across the state (Lockdown 3 ended).

18: I received a letter from Victoria's new A-G in response to my letter of 24 August 2020 to the previous A-G.

March 2021

19: I had a telehealth session with a psychologist as part of the process for participation in EFHAS.

24–25: I travelled to Adelaide for the purpose of filming the introduction of my story with EFHAS.

31: AIS informed me that there continued to be no response from my brothers in Greece to their outreaches.

April 2021

06: Victoria's new BDM Registrar phoned me indicating BDM would do all it could within the relevant legislation to assist me. I clarified the legal questions to which I was seeking answers from the Department.

14: I met with BDM to discuss my case.

29: I finished my employment with Jesuit Social Services, having given notice on 1 April 2021.

May 2021

12: The Victorian Government announced plans to make it easier for Victorians to become parents by establishing the first public IVF service and public sperm and egg bank in Victoria.[188]

19: I received a letter from BDM confirming our discussion at our meeting of 14 April 2021, and indicating that BDM was seeking further legal advice regarding the current status of my adoption.

28: The Victorian Government imposed snap Stage 4 COVID-19 restrictions across the state (Lockdown 4 commenced). The restrictions were eased in Regional Victoria from 3 June 2021.

31: I requested an update on the progress of the legal advice being sought by BDM.

---

188 See Martin Foley (12 May 2021) 'Public IVF To Make Starting A Family Easier For Victorians'.

June 2021

01: I was informed that BDM had "now corrected" my pre-adoptive birth certificate leaving the 'Mother' field blank.

10: The Victorian Government lifted the Stage 4 COVID-19 restrictions across Metropolitan Melbourne (Lockdown 4 ended).

11: I informed BDM that my "corrected" pre-adoptive birth certificate had not arrived via post, and subsequently collected it from the BDM office later the same day.

15: I asked BDM when the legal advice regarding the status of my adoption was anticipated and the BDM Registrar agreed to follow up.

21: I had my seventh session with the private counsellor.

29: I received an email with a "précis" of the VGSO's advice provided to the BDM Registrar, which stated "the department's position" that my adoption was legally valid. I requested the grounds on which this legal position was reached.

July 2021

02: BDM informed me that the VGSO was reluctant to provide the details of its legal position to me, and that BDM would meet with the VGSO on 5 July 2021 to discuss the matter.

05: BDM informed me about their meeting with the VGSO that day—the VGSO initially advised they were "not in a position to provide any further information", but later claimed "client privilege" whereby the DJCS was their client, not me.

07: I phoned the County Court to clarify the documents required to apply for discharge of an Adoption Order and confirmed the lodgement fee of $500.50.

09: The BDM Registrar informed me that the VGSO was willing to reconsider the details of my case, and that they would meet the following week to discuss the matter further.

13: Following her meeting with the VGSO, the BDM Registrar informed me that the VGSO was now reviewing my case.

16: The Victorian Government imposed snap Stage 4 COVID-19 restrictions across the state (Lockdown 5 commenced).

26: I discussed with AIS my planned application to the County Court for discharge of my Adoption Order, reclamation and integration of my true original identity, and correction of my official records.

27: The Victorian Government lifted the Stage 4 COVID-19 restrictions across the state (Lockdown 5 ended).

August 2021

Integrated birth certificates became available to adopted persons in the ACT subsequent to passage of the *Births, Deaths and Marriages Registration Amendment Bill 2020*.[189]

05: The Victorian Government imposed snap Stage 4 COVID-19 restrictions across the state (Lockdown 6 commenced).

06: I engaged Macpherson Kelley solicitors to review and refine the draft documents I had prepared for my application to the County Court, and to assist in seeking a formal apology from Monash Health for what happened to me at the QVMH and their destruction of my hospital records.

13: BDM informed me that the VGSO had completed its review and that their initial advice stood.

13: I lodged an Application to Discharge my Adoption Order under s.19(1)(B) of the *Adoption Act 1984* with the County Court of Victoria.

24: The County Court confirmed receipt of my adoption discharge application.

September 2021

08: The Report from the Parliamentary Inquiry into Responses to Historical Forced Adoptions in Victoria was tabled in the Victorian Parliament.[190] The Report made 56 recommendations, mainly focused on the experience of mothers, although several recommendations directly concern adopted people—such as the introduction of "integrated birth certificates without delay, issued to people who are

---

189 See Access Canberra (2021) 'Integrated Birth Certificate Factsheet'.

190 See Parliament of Victoria (2021) 'Report tabled, Inquiry into Responses to Historical Forced Adoptions in Victoria'.

adopted upon request" (#26); and the introduction of "a no-fault, no-fee procedure for applications to discharge an adoption order" (#16).

20: In a series of articles relating to the 2021 AFL Finals Series published in *The Age* about supporters of the Melbourne Football Club, Martin Flanagan wrote about me, including the revelation of my Greek ancestry and having had my identity swapped in hospital soon after birth.[191]

28: A County Court Registrar contacted me seeking clarification in relation to my application.

29: Macpherson Kelley sent a letter to Monash Health on my behalf requesting a formal apology by 13 October 2021 for their wrongful actions of the past and acknowledgement of the consequences. Monash Health's Chief Legal Officer replied, expressing concern that the letter accused Monash Health of having engaged in illegal conduct.

October 2021

06–07: Macpherson Kelly replied to Monash Health, forwarding copies of relevant documents.

11: AIS discussed with me an option suggested by Her Honour Judge Davis to only correct and annotate the relevant records on the Birth and Adoption Registers, rather than also discharge my Adoption Order and change my legal identity.

12: I emailed the County Court confirming I had thoroughly read the relevant sections of the *Births, Deaths and Marriages Registration Act 1996* suggested by Her Honour, and that I continued to seek discharge of my Adoption Order to correct the historic details recorded about me on the relevant Registers and to integrate the correct details with my legal identity.

21: Macpherson Kelley received a letter from Monash Health indicating it was unable to find any further information regarding my QVMH records than it had previously provided, and reiterated Monash Health's position that destruction of my medical records was

---

191 See Martin Flanagan (20 September 2021) 'Penny Mackieson'.

permitted under the Public Record Office disposal schedule in place at the time. No apology was offered.

22: The Victorian Government lifted the Stage 4 COVID-19 restrictions across the state (Lockdown 6 ended).

28: AIS informed me that the County Court had now officially requested a report in relation to my application for discharge of my Adoption Order.

November 2021

07: I contacted the sailing company in Greece to enquire about re-booking our chartered yacht cruise around the Small Cyclades for July-August 2022.

08: I had a long meeting with AIS as part of the process for preparation of its report to the County Court in relation to my application to discharge my Adoption Order.

16: I confirmed our booking with the sailing company in Greece.

18: The AIS Manager informed me that AIS's report was awaiting finalisation by a senior manager before it could be submitted to the County Court.

18: EFHAS contacted me requesting my permission to upload my DNA data to GEDmatch, FamilyTreeDNA and MyHeritage, to which I agreed.

23: I requested that Flight Centre book flights and make other arrangements for Bruce, Patrick and me to visit Scotland and Greece in June-August 2022.

December 2021

01: I paid for our flights, car hire and travel insurance for our planned trip to Scotland and Greece.

January 2022

10–14: I attended a Summer School at the Hellenic Museum in Melbourne on the 'History and culture of the ancient world'.

February 2022

03: I contacted the County Court enquiring about the progress of my adoption discharge application, which was now before Her Honour.

14: I was informed that Her Honour was reviewing my application and had invited Donna to make a submission by 22 February 2022 regarding any objection she may have had to an order to correct the Registers.

23: I contacted the County Court to check whether Donna had lodged any objection to the orders I sought and whether a hearing date had been scheduled.

28: I enquired to the County Court about the scheduling of a hearing for my application and was informed that the court intended to hold a hearing remotely the following week.

March 2022

08: I enquired again to the County Court about the scheduling of a hearing.

09: The County Court informed me that a hearing (via Zoom) had been listed for midday on 15 March 2022.

10: The Victorian Government's Response to the recommendations of the Parliamentary *Inquiry into Responses to Historical Forced Adoption in Victoria* was tabled in the Victorian Parliament.[192]

10: The Victorian Government announced an allocation of more than $4 million in response to the *Inquiry into Responses to Historical Forced Adoption in Victoria*, including for:

- planning "to design and establish Australia's first redress scheme for … women who gave birth between 1958 and 1984 and were subjected to cruel and damaging forced adoption practices,"[193] expected to be completed by July 2023. Meanwhile, the Government established a $500,000 hardship fund for "mothers affected by forced adoption between 1958 and 1984 who have exceptional circumstances," with applications to open on 1 July 2022;[194] and

---

192 See Victorian Government (2022) *Victorian Government Response to the Recommendations of the Legislative Assembly Legal and Social Issues Committee's Inquiry into Responses to Historical Forced Adoptions in Victoria*.

193 Quoted from Daniel Andrews and Jaclyn Symes (10 March 2022). Op. cit.

194 Quoted from Justice and Community Safety (2022) 'Forced Adoption Exceptional Circumstances Fund'.

- introducing "the option of integrated birth certificates which include the names of both the adopted person's natural parents and their adoptive parents."[195]

11: The County Court informed me that Her Honour did not object to my request for particular family members, friends and a journalist to attend the closed court hearing scheduled for 15 March 2022.

15: In a brief hearing of the County Court of Victoria (held remotely via Zoom), Her Honour Judge Davis made orders in accordance with my Application that

- discharged my Adoption Order;
- corrected the registrable information contained in the pre-adoptive entry in the Register about my birth; and
- changed my name to Penny xxx Zagarelou-Mackieson.[196]

The court also made orders of its own motion that corrected the registrable information contained in the pre-adoptive entry about Donna's birth.

15: Gus McCubbing, the journalist who attended my County Court hearing, reported on the story of my journey to integrate my true identity.[197]

16: I advised the County Court of a date correction required to my Discharge of Adoption Order.

16: AIS forwarded me a copy of the report it prepared in relation to my County Court application.

18: Dee Dee Dunleavy interviewed me on Radio 3AW regarding the discovery that I was swapped soon after birth before having been adopted and the Victorian Government's announcement of a redress scheme for mothers.

21: The County Court sent me a corrected Discharge of Adoption Order. However, the year on the corrected order was still wrong.

---

195 Quoted from Daniel Andrews and Jaclyn Symes (10 March 2022). Op. cit.
196 "xxx" denotes my original first name, which I have chosen not to disclose.
197 See Gus McCubbing's article in *The Ararat Advertiser*, 'Adoptee's 33-year Journey to 'Right' Name' (15 March 2022). The story was also reported by numerous other media outlets including, for example, Australian Associated Press (15 March 2022) '"I Never Felt Right": DNA Test Reveals Melbourne Woman Introduced to Wrong "Biological Mother"'.

22: The County Court sent me a second corrected Discharge of Adoption Order. Later the same day, the court sent me a third corrected Discharge of Adoption Order and a corrected Correction of Registrable Information Order because the wrong court reference number was originally printed on both orders.

25: The Associate forwarded me a copy of Her Honour's Reasons for Decision and a copy of AIS's report.

25: I replied to the Associate raising that the Reasons for Decision stated I was "inadvertently swapped with another baby." However, investigations had been unable to determine whether my having been swapped was accidental or intentional. Therefore, for accuracy, I requested that Her Honour delete the word "inadvertently."

25: I received a copy of my new birth certificate from BDM, consequent to the orders made in the County Court on 15 March 2022.

25: I emailed the BDM Registrar raising two linked details on the front of my new birth certificate which I believed should also be corrected in accordance with the orders: my birth Registration Number, and the Date of Registration.

27: I emailed the BDM Registrar raising concerns with one of the two history notes recorded on the back of my new birth certificate.

31: Her Honour's Associate forwarded me a copy of the Reasons for Decision amended in accordance with my email of 25 March 2022.

31: I met with the Registrar of BDM, the BDM Operations Manager and the Deputy Director, Adoption Services, to discuss the details to be printed on my new birth certificate. We agreed that the best way to proceed was for BDM to re-register my birth from scratch.

April 2022

04: I received my new birth certificate, amended in accordance with the decisions agreed with BDM on 31 March 2022.

05: The Victorian Government announced the introduction to Parliament of legislation to "create integrated birth certificates, allowing the names of an adopted person's birth parents, adoptive parents and the date of their adoption to be included on their certificate ... for adopted people aged 18 years and older."[198] This was purportedly in response to the Parliamentary Inquiry into Responses to Historical Forced Adoptions in Victoria (Recommendation #26).[199]

19: I received my new Australian passport, issued in accordance with my new legal identity.

May 2022

07: Bruce, Patrick and I held an event for 50 family members and friends at Bahari, a Greek restaurant in Melbourne, to celebrate formal recognition of my true origins and new integrated legal identity. (The invitation to the celebration is provided at Appendix I, and the speech I gave at the event is provided at Appendix II.)

31: The Victorian Parliament's omnibus legislation, the *Justice Legislation Amendment Bill 2022*,[200] received assent.[201] This legislation provides for the implementation of optional integrated birth certificates for adults adopted in Victoria, expected to be available by late 2023.[202]

June 2022

A second request was made to Monash Health for a formal apology, this time via personal outreach to the Chief Executive by a former colleague and good friend, Jenny McAuley, advocating on my behalf.

27: Bruce, Patrick and I departed Melbourne for Edinburgh, Scotland (UK).

30: I travelled to London by train to visit Professor Gonda Van Steen, stayed overnight and returned to Edinburgh the next day.

July 2022

12: Bruce, Patrick and I departed Edinburgh for Athens, where we stayed two nights before driving to Nafplio in Western Greece.

---

198 Quoted from Jaclyn Symes (5 April 2022). Op. cit.

199 The introduction of integrated birth certificates was previously recommended in 2017 by the VLRC following its *Review of the Adoption Act* 1984, and earlier (in 2012) by the Senate following its Inquiry into the Commonwealth contribution to former forced adoption policies and practices.

200 See Parliament of Victoria (2022) 'Justice Legislation Amendment Bill 2022'.

201 See Victorian Government (2022) 'Victorian Legislation, Justice Legislation Amendment Bill 2022'.

202 See Jaclyn Symes (5 April 2022). Op. cit.

20: Bruce, Patrick and I drove back from Nafplio to Athens. Bruce and Patrick then left for Melbourne. I was joined a few days later by my good friend, Catherine Neville. After a few more days in Athens, we ferried to Paros where we were joined by my good friends, Veronica Sakell and her husband Bruce Gemmell, and departed on a chartered yacht cruise around the Small Cyclades. Catherine and I then ferried to Santorini for a few days before returning to Athens.

August 2022

10: Catherine and I departed Athens for Melbourne.

25: I met with AIS and requested they outreach directly to my brother, Nikos, who we believed ran a business in the town where he and our mother, Georgia, reside in Greece. Accordingly, AIS agreed to send a letter in Greek to Nikos.

September 2022

05: I contacted McKean Park Lawyers seeking copies of any records relating to Georgia, my birth, and my adoption that may have been held by the firm.

07: McKean Park Lawyers advised that any paper file containing information about my adoption would have been destroyed after 1988.

15: I wrote to the Board of Monash Health requesting a formal apology for wrongs done to me at the QVMH in 1963. (My letter is provided at Appendix III.)

October 2022

04: The AIS Manager informed me there had been no response to the letter sent to Nikos at his business in Greece, and that I have a third sibling—a younger sister, Sofia.[203]

06: The AIS Manager informed me she had spoken with Nikos at his business in Greece and discovered he is actually a cousin with the same name as my brother.

11: The AIS Manager informed me she'd had a phone conversation with my brother, Nikos, and had told him there is someone in Melbourne

---

203 "Sofia" is an alias first name.

AIS believes is his older sister. Nikos requested that the AIS Manager phone him again in two weeks' time, so he could inform his two younger siblings and discuss the matter with them in the meantime.

12: The Victorian Government announced its intention to "establish a redress scheme, provide support and deliver a formal apology to Victorians who were placed in orphanages, children's homes and missions and experienced physical, psychological and emotional abuse or neglect."[204] The announcement included that $2.9 million would be spent on co-designing the scheme (to cover the period between 1928 and 1990), "which will include urgent hardship payments of up to $10,000 for care leavers in exceptional circumstances." The media release reiterated that "The Government has invested more than $4 million in response to last year's *Parliamentary Inquiry into Historical Forced Adoption in Victoria,* including a plan to co-design and establish Australia's first redress scheme for people affected by forced adoption."

24–26: I participated in filming with EFHAS.

25: In an interview with medical historian, Dr Madonna Grehan, I was informed that 18 months of QVMH medical records had been completely destroyed, including all of those for 1963.

26 (morning): In an interview with Jason Reeve from AncestryDNA, I was informed that, although there were still no close relative matches, the results for my distant relative matches are consistent with Georgia being my natural mother.

26: The AIS Manager informed me about phone calls she'd had the previous day with my brothers, Nikos and Yiannis,[205] in Greece. They indicated that all three siblings wished to proceed with DNA testing to clarify our relationships and, subsequently, to meet me.

November 2022

14: I received a letter of apology from Monash Health (which is provided at Appendix IV).

---

204 Quoted from Daniel Andrews and Colin Brooks (12 October 2022) 'Past Care Leavers: We Hear You'.
205 "Yiannis" is an alias first name.

18: I was a guest speaker and panellist at VANISH's AGM on the topic 'Adoption Deception to Donor Conception'. (My speech is presented in Appendix V.)

March 2023

08: Jason Reeve from AncestryDNA informed me of the results of the AncestryDNA tests taken by my putative siblings in Greece, which confirmed that we are maternal half-siblings.

15: I had my first phone conversation (facilitated by the AIS Manager) with Yiannis, one of my maternal brothers, in Greece.

21: As a member of the VANISH contingent invited to Canberra by the Commonwealth Government, I attended two events to commemorate the 10th Anniversary of the National Apology for Forced Adoptions:
- a panel discussion, 'Saying sorry: do national apologies change the world?', held at the National Archives of Australia; and
- a Commemoration Dinner held at the National Portrait Gallery.[206]

22: As a member of the VANISH contingent invited to Canberra by the Commonwealth Government, I attended the House of Representatives gallery to hear a statement on the significant matter of the 10th Anniversary of the National Apology for Forced Adoptions by Social Services Minister, Amanda Rishworth,[207] and a response by Shadow Social Services Minister, Michael Sukkar,[208] followed by a morning tea, at Parliament House, Canberra.

26: I had my second phone conversation (facilitated by the AIS Manager) with Yiannis in Greece.

April 2023

02: I had my first direct conversation (via phone and Viber) with my sister Sofia, and brother Yiannis, in Greece.

---

206 See Department of Social Services (29 March 2023) 'Tenth Anniversary of the National Apology for Forced Adoptions, 21 March 2013'.

207 See Amanda Rishworth's media release of 21 March 2023, 'Government Marks Ten Year Anniversary of the National Apology for Forced Adoptions'.

208 See Michael Sukkar's media release of 22 March 2023, 'Statement: National Apology for Forced Adoption—Tenth Anniversary'.

POSTSCRIPT

I am still on a high. It has been two weeks since I returned from my second trip to Greece. As anticipated, the trip involved many firsts: meeting my mother, Georgia, for the first time since my birth; meeting my three maternal siblings, Nikos, Yiannis and Sofia, for the first time ever in person; and likewise meeting my maternal aunt and uncle. These meetings went way better than I had dared to imagine, even though I had grounds for high hopes. First, because Yiannis had expressed before I left for Greece that my siblings were determined I would meet our mother on this trip, and he and Sofia worked hard to ensure that it happened. Also, because only a few days before departing Melbourne with my friends, Jenny and Catherine, a maternal cousin living in Melbourne contacted me and warmly welcomed me to the family.

I am still processing all the interactions with my family members, the information shared with me regarding our history, and the family dynamics. Nevertheless, I am aware of a deep contentment permeating my mind and body since registering not only that I have found my true tribe but that they accept me and have embraced me, just as I have for so long sought to embrace them. Perhaps it is a sense of completeness, or how it feels to have healed. Regardless, it is something for which I am deeply grateful.

On the other hand, I am still figuring out how to accurately portray meeting my family without it appearing over-sentimental; without it reading like the closing chapter or scene of the sort of novel or movie I mentioned in the Introduction. I have long despised schmaltzy, happily-ever-after, fairy-tale endings to adoption reunion stories because such depiction is merely a snapshot in time. I know from direct experience that post-reunion 'honeymoon' relationships are complex to maintain due to the lack of shared history growing up and associated absence of deeply integrated understandings of each other. I also know that such relationships can deteriorate quickly following seemingly innocuous exchanges. My newfound elation is thus constantly tempered by mindfulness of the potential for things to evolve less positively for me and my family, and of the unfairness that other individuals who discover they were misidentified before their adoption may not find themselves in as fortunate a position as we are. And I do feel fortunate—as if the sliding doors of deception and confusion associated with my early misidentification and adoption have been securely closed behind me.

As recently as 2019, I had reasons to believe that I may never get to meet any of my family in Greece. So, our recent family reunion is extremely personal and precious to me, as are the individuals involved and our fledgling social relationships. I have thus chosen to not disclose the details of our meetings here for the same reason I chose not to share them on camera with *Every Family Has A Secret* (EFHAS), grateful though I am for their assistance in conjunction with AncestryDNA for the purpose of helping me to connect with my family.

It must suffice here to report that I had multiple meetings over coffee and meals with various family members in Greece and we exchanged gifts. I experienced our interactions as mutually warm, affectionate and genuine, and contact has continued since my return home to Melbourne. I saw first-hand many strong resemblances between me and Georgia and other maternal family members in regard to our personalities, interests and passions, as well as physically and intellectually. Most powerfully, during my first meeting with Georgia, she expressed—despite the communication difficulties associated with her speaking little English and me speaking little Greek—that she has always loved me and constantly thought about me. I enthusiastically committed to returning to Greece soon with Bruce and Patrick to visit my family again, about which we are all excited. I also promised Georgia that I will by then have learned sufficient Greek language to be able to have full conversations directly with her, rather than through someone else translating for us. There are many things we wish to discuss with each other in private.

Notwithstanding the good foundations now laid for positive ongoing relationships, my family reunion in Greece was, in fact, decades in the making. I have been actively seeking information about, and subsequently contact with, my family for 34 years. I made this point to several family members in the context of explaining why and how I had sought to connect with them. The revelation through DNA testing that I was misidentified soon after birth, which dramatically hijacked and delayed our reunion, has not been easy for anyone to grasp. And while I have dedicated years to dealing with the aftermath, it is a comparatively new piece of information for several of my family members to digest. In any event, I recognise that I will need to continue taking care in navigating our geographic, cultural, religious, education, lifestyle and language differences moving forward. I have already had to consider the potential impact of my activism in relation to adoption in Australia and subsequently discussed my books and involvement with EFHAS with family members in Greece.

I am now in a much better headspace than during the first years after discovering that my identity was swapped with another baby's soon after birth. Assisted by some expert professionals and supportive family members and close friends, I eventually succeeded in navigating the aftermath of that unanticipated revelation. It is a huge relief, as well as the fulfilment of a lifelong desire, to know for sure where I came from and, especially, from whom I came. I am in no doubt that this will help me deal with whatever else life may throw at me in the future. Meanwhile, I realise that other people may deal with such a situation in different ways to those that I chose. Nevertheless, I sincerely hope that the sharing of my story in this book will provide fuel for those who seek the truth of their own origins. Success does not happen without perseverance, and perseverance cannot happen without hope.

ABBREVIATIONS

....

AASW   Australian Association of Social Workers

ACT   Australian Capital Territory

A-G   Attorney-General

AGM   Annual General Meeting

AHPRA   Australian Health Practitioner Regulation Agency

AIHW   Australian Institute of Health and Welfare

AIS   Adoption Information Service:

Delivered through the Victorian Government's Adoption Services, Department of Justice and Community Safety (DJCS) since 1 July 2019 when responsibility for Victoria's adoption services transferred from the Department of Health and Human Services (DHHS).

Adoption Services includes local adoption, intercountry adoption, information about past adoptions, and adoption relinquishment counselling.

ART   Assisted Reproductive Technology

BDM   Department of Births, Deaths and Marriages (Victorian Government)

BDM Act   *Births, Deaths and Marriages Registration Act 1996* (Vic)

CAE   Council of Adult Education

CBD   Central Business District

CCYP   Commission for Children and Young People (Victoria)

CYFA   *Children, Youth and Families Act 2005* (Vic)

DHHS   Department of Health and Human Services, a former department of the Victorian Government.

DJCS   Department of Justice and Community Safety (Victorian Government)

DNA	DNA is the abbreviation for deoxyribonucleic acid, an organic chemical of complex molecular structure that is found in all prokaryotic and eukaryotic cells and in many viruses. DNA codes genetic information for the transmission of inherited traits.[209]
EFHAS	*Every Family Has A Secret*: A TV series produced by Artemis Media for SBS.[210]
FIND	Family Information Networks and Discovery: The Victorian Government's Adoption Information Service (AIS) was known as FIND when delivered by the DHHS. Since July 2019, AIS has been delivered by the DJCS.
FOI	Freedom of Information
IBC	Integrated birth certificate (*see Glossary*)
ICAR	International Conference on Adoption Research
MRI	Magnetic Resonance Imaging: A medical imaging technique that takes detailed pictures of the inside of the body for diagnostic and treatment purposes.
NZ	New Zealand
NSW	New South Wales
OOHC	Out of home (or out-of-home) care: Alternative care for a child or young person in the context of the child protection system. Alternative care options include foster care, kinship care, residential care, permanent care, etc.
PCO	Permanent Care Order (Victoria): "An order granting permanent guardianship and custody of a child to a third party. Unlike adoption orders, permanent care orders do not change the legal status of the child, and they expire when the child turns 18 or marries. An application may be made to revoke or amend a permanent care order."[211]
PhD	Doctor of Philosophy
QVH	Queen Victoria Hospital: A shorter version of the Queen Victoria Memorial Hospital (QVMH). *Also, see below for 'QVMH'.*
QVMH	Queen Victoria Memorial Hospital, Lonsdale Street, Melbourne:

---

209 See Britannica (2023) 'DNA chemical compound'.
210 See Artemis Media (2022). Op. cit.; and SBS (2022). Op. cit.
211 Quoted from Australian Institute of Health and Welfare (2017). Op. cit.

The hospital was acquired by Monash Health in 1987. In its heyday, the QVMH was the second largest women's hospital, and had the second largest infant adoption program, in the state of Victoria.

RWH   Royal Women's Hospital (Melbourne)

SA   South Australia

SBS   Special Broadcasting Service:

"an Australian hybrid-funded public service broadcaster. About 80 percent of funding for the company is derived from the Australian Government ... The stated purpose of SBS is 'to provide multilingual and multicultural radio and television services that inform, educate and entertain all Australians and, in doing so, reflect Australia's multicultural society.' SBS is one of five main free-to-air networks in Australia."[212]

"SBS is a modern, multiplatform media organisation with a free-to-air TV portfolio spanning six distinctive channels in SBS, NITV, SBS VICELAND, SBS Food, SBS World Movies and SBS WorldWatch; an extensive radio network providing over 60 communities with services in their own language; and an innovative digital offering, including SBS On Demand, available to audiences anytime and anywhere."[213]

UK   United Kingdom

USA   United States of America

VANISH, VANISH Inc.

The organisation formerly known as the Victorian Adoption Network for Information and Self Help.[214]

VGSO   Victorian Government Solicitor's Office

Vic   Victoria

VLRC   Victorian Law Reform Commission

---

212 Quoted from Wikipedia (2022) 'Special Broadcasting Service'.
213 Quoted from SBS (2020) 'Who We Are'.
214 See VANISH Inc. (2022). Op. cit.

GLOSSARY

adoptee   A person who is the subject of an Adoption Order. May also be referred to as an adopted child, adopted adult, or adopted person.

adoption   A "legal process involving the transfer of the rights and responsibilities for the permanent care of a child from the child's parent(s) to their adoptive parent(s). The legal relationship between the child and the parent(s) is severed, and any legal rights that existed from birth regarding the birth parent(s)—such as inheritance—are removed. For the adoptive parents, the legal rights of the adopted child become the same as they would be if the child had been born to the adoptive parent(s)."[215]

adoption discharge   *See 'discharge of adoption' below.*

adoption microaggression   "The construct of microaggressions, including microassaults, microinvalidations, and microinsults, as well as a new construct (developed for the ... framework of adoption microaggressions) called microfictions (the mistruths and stories created about adoption that deny and misrepresent real, lived adoption experience), can be applied to communication about the practice of adoption, adoption status, adoptive parenting, being a birth parent, and being an adopted person, as well as other adoption-related concerns."[216] *See also 'microaggression' below.*

Adoption Order   "A judicial or administrative order, made by a competent authority under adoption legislation, by which the adoptive parent(s) become the legal parent(s) of the child."[217]

---

215 Quoted from Australian Institute of Health and Welfare (2021) *Child Protection Australia 2019–20*, p. 85.
216 Quoted from Amanda Baden (2016). Op. cit., p. 6.
217 Quoted from Australian Institute of Health and Welfare (2021) 'Adoptions, Glossary'.

adoptive parent   "A person who has become the parent of a child or adult as the result of an adoption order."[218]

alternative care   The term now often used instead of out-of-home care in the context of the child protection system. Alternative care options include foster care, kinship care, residential care, permanent care, etc.

closed adoption   "Adoption arrangements involving no further contact between the natural parents and the child after legalisation of the adoption, often also involving the permanent sealing of the adoptee's original birth records for the purposes of maintaining secrecy."[219]

coercive adoption   An adoption "arranged under policies or practices associated with either of the following contexts:

- adoption in the context of former (i.e., pre-1980s) 'forced adoption' policies and practices in Australia for which all respective state, territory and national governments have formally apologised; or
- adoption in the child protection context, where the child has generally been removed from their parents involuntarily and, especially, when the adoption of the child is pursued through legal dispensation of the requirement for the child's parents to give their informed and duress-free consent."[220]

consumer genetic genealogy test   A DNA-based test used in genetic genealogy that is available commercially to individual consumers. Such a test finds or verifies ancestral genealogical relationships, or (with lower reliability) estimates a person's ethnic heritage.[221] Companies that provide consumer genetic genealogy tests include, for example, AncestryDNA, GEDmatch, Living DNA, MyHeritage, and 23andMe.

de-adopted, de-adoption   De-adoption is the undoing of a previously legally finalised adoption, as defined in 1988 by psychiatrists Paul L. Adams and Ivan Fras.[222] To be de-adopted is different to being unadopted, because being unadopted means not having been adopted in the first place.[223]

---

218 Ibid.
219 Quoted from Penny Mackieson (2019). Op. cit., p. ix.
220 Ibid, p. ix.
221 See International Society of Genetic Genealogy Wiki (2022). Op. cit.; and, also, the Wikipedia entry for 'Genealogical DNA Test' (2022).
222 See p. 494 of Paul Adams and Ivan Fras' book, *Beginning Child Psychiatry* (1988).
223 Collins Dictionary (2022) 'Definition of "Unadopted".

discharge of adoption   A Discharge of Adoption Order is a court order that undoes the legal effect of an Adoption Order. The "adoption ceases to exist and the person is no longer an adopted person or legally connected to the family that adopted them. They become legally reconnected to their birth family." For Adoption Orders granted in the state of Victoria, Australia, an application for Discharge of the Adoption Order must be made to the County Court of Victoria.[224]

forced adoption   A form of coercive adoption (*see above*):
"… policies and practices resulting in forced adoptions were widespread throughout Australia in the post-[Second World-]war period … It occurred when children were given up for adoption because their parents, particularly their mothers, were forced to relinquish them or faced circumstances in which they were left with no other choice … between the late 1950s and the mid-1970s."[225]

foster care   "A form of out-of-home care where the caregiver is authorised and reimbursed (or was offered but declined reimbursement) by the state/territory for the care of the child. This category excludes relatives/kin who are reimbursed. There are varying degrees of reimbursement made to foster carers."[226]

fosterage   The practice in Ancient Greece of taking in an orphaned or abandoned child and raising it as a natural child, not as a slave:
"Fosterage gave the orphaned or abandoned child a new home but did not involve any change in filiation or status. It was mainly concerned with the child's welfare."[227]

full adoption   See 'plenary adoption' below.

integrated birth certificate   An official birth certificate (i.e., primary legal identity document) that records the details of an adopted person's natural parents as well as the details of their adoptive parents.

kinship care, relative/kinship care   "A form of out-of-home care where the caregiver is:
- a relative (other than parents)
- considered to be family or a close friend

---

224 Quoted from Department of Justice and Community Safety (2022) 'Discharge of Adoption'.

225 Quoted from Senate Community Affairs References Committee (2012). Op. cit., p. 4.

226 Quoted from Australian Institute of Health and Welfare (2018) *Child protection Australia 2016–17*. Op. cit., p. 74.

227 Quoted from Sabine R. Huebner (2013). Op. cit., p. 510.

- a member of the child or young person's community (in accordance with their culture).

For Aboriginal and Torres Strait Islander children, a kinship carer may be another Indigenous person who is a member of their community, a compatible community, or from the same language group."[228]

known child adoption   "An adoption of a child/children who were born or permanently living in Australia before the adoption, who have a pre-existing relationship with the adoptive parent(s), and who are generally not able to be adopted by anyone other than the adoptive parent(s). These types of adoptions are broken down into the following categories, depending on the child's relationship to the adoptive parent(s): step-parent, relative(s), carer and other."[229]

microaggression   The "subtle forms of racism … evident in modern life … attitudes, judgments, prejudice, and racism that are communicated in subtle, overt, and sometimes aggressive ways in everyday life."[230]
See also 'adoption microaggression' above.

mother   A person's natural mother (i.e., biological and genetic female parent), unless otherwise specified: for example, adoptive mother, stepmother, foster mother, etc.

natural (relative)   A biologically or genetically related person.

open adoption   An adoption involving arrangements for "ongoing contact between the child and their natural parents after legalisation of the child's adoption, usually including legal access for the adopted person to their original birth records at the age of 18 years (or earlier by agreement with the parties involved)."[231]

plenary adoption   Also known as full adoption, the generic social construct of adoption commonly used in Western societies (i.e., Australia, Canada, Ireland, New Zealand, the UK, and the USA).
As described above for 'adoption'.

putative (relative)   A person who is officially recognised as, or presumed to be, a natural relative.

---

228 Quoted from Australian Institute of Health and Welfare (2021) *Child Protection Australia 2019–20*. Op. cit., p. 91.
229 Quoted from Australian Institute of Health and Welfare (2021) 'Adoptions, Glossary'. Op. cit.
230 Quoted from Amanda Baden (2016). Op. cit., p. 5.
231 Quoted from Penny Mackieson (2019). Op. cit., p. xii.

simple adoption　An adoption recognised in law in countries including France, Romania, Japan, Thailand, and many countries in South America (e.g., Brazil) and Africa (e.g., Ethiopia). Simple adoption is often used in a step-parent context because it does not completely sever the legal relationships between the natural parents and the child. Simple adoption vests day-today responsibilities for parenting in the adoptive parent(s), while retaining the fundamental legal aspects of the relationships between the natural parents and adopted child.[232]

In Australia, only plenary or full adoptions are legally recognised (and not 'simple adoptions').

232　See Kerry O'Halloran (2021). Op. cit., pp. 4–6, and 158–159; and Karleen Gribble and Stacy Blythe (28 November 2019). Op. cit.

APPENDIX I

Invitation to the celebration, May 2022

Please join us to celebrate the formal recognition
of Penny's true origins and her new integrated legal identity!

Penny   **Zagarelou-Mackieson**

From 1–4pm on Saturday 7 May 2022
Upstairs at Bahari
179 Swan Street, Richmond, Victoria
(enter from door at left, NOT main front door to the restaurant)

Please RSVP by 22 April 2022

APPENDIX II

My speech at the celebration, May 2022

Καλησπέρα, κυρίες και κύριοι! Σας ευχαριστώ που ήρθατε σήμερα.

I hope what I've just said in Greek is: "Good afternoon, ladies and gentlemen. Thank you for coming today", and not: "I saw Nick Kyrgios yesterday, and he was doing a poo."

We're here to celebrate something quite unusual, so I truly appreciate all your efforts to join us—especially my friends Veronica and Bruce who've made a special trip from Hobart, and David and Min who've travelled from Apollo Bay, and my brother Peter and his partner Veronica who've come from Bairnsdale.

I must admit it was Bruce who suggested having this get together to celebrate *my new legal identity*. My friend Sinead has called it a *naming ceremony*, but that doesn't feel quite right to me, as I've had to steal my own thunder by announcing my new name in advance, so it could be legalised.

Nevertheless, it seems an appropriate occasion for κουφέτα (Greek for sugared almonds), so you must take home some μπομπονιέρα.

I had wanted to wait for this get together until after my first trip to Greece, which was postponed from 2020 due to the COVID-19 pandemic but is now to happen in July-August. I thought I might feel more *Greekified* once I've been there.

But I'm glad Bruce insisted on holding it now because it's made me pause, smell the coffee, and reflect on how much dealing with the revelation of my Greek origins has dominated my life *and*, consequently, how much it's impacted those close to me. Hopefully, this celebration will help bring closure and enable me, and us, to move on.

I thought it may be useful if I briefly explain how and why my new legal identity has come about. It's complicated and a lot to take in, so I'll summarise:

1. What I've done
2. Why I've done it, and
3. What it means going forward

1. What is it that I've done?

I lodged an application with the County Court of Victoria in August last year, which was resolved at a hearing held on the 15th of March this year.

It was actually my second application to the County Court—the first was lodged in December 2019, and successfully resolved in July 2020, to obtain identifying information about my real biological mother.

As requested in my second application to the County Court, at the hearing in March, the Judge granted several orders which did three key things:

  i. **Discharged my Adoption Order**

  My Adoption Order was granted in the County Court in Bairnsdale in May 1964, more than a year after I was born and placed at three weeks of age with my beloved Dad and Mum—my adoptive parents, the late Lionel and Lois Mackieson.

  ii. **Correctly recognised me as the person born xxx Zagarelou**

  On Victoria's official Birth and Adoption Registers, as well as on my Adoption Order, my original identity is incorrectly recorded as the person born **** **** *****. It was critical that I be legally recognised as the person born xxx Zagarelou, otherwise the discharge of my Adoption Order would have resulted in my legal identity automatically reverting to **** **** *****.

iii. **Authorised BDM to issue a new official Birth Certificate for me**, which:

- Records the identity of the Greek mother to whom I was actually born, and the name she gave me at birth; and
- Formalises my new legal identity, which integrates my true original name with my adoptive name. So, my legal name has changed from *Penelope Kathleen Mackieson* to *Penny xxx Zagarelou-Mackieson*. I took the opportunity to legally change my first name to its diminutive because I've *never* liked the formality of "Penelope"—never mind that it's a Greek name—and besides, I've always been known to everyone as "Penny").

2. So, why did I make the second application to the County Court?

Because, after much exploration and consideration, seeking discharge of my adoption was the only avenue that enabled legal correction of the birth and adoption records, and formal integration of my true origins and identity.

As most of you probably know, in 2016, I inadvertently began to discover, through the results of an AncestryDNA test, that I was misidentified prior to being placed with the Mackieson family. The biggest clue was not that over half the names of the people identified as my DNA relatives were Greek, but that my DNA includes *0% Anglo-Celtic ethnicity* and had *70% Greek ethnicity*.

I concluded that both of my biological parents must be Greek, and strongly suspected that the Anglo-Welsh mother on my birth and adoption records *with whom I'd been in reunion since 1997* was genetically unrelated to me.

Since 2019, when my misidentification was acknowledged by the Victorian Government's Adoption Information Service (the 'AIS'), it's been extremely important to me to have the official records corrected.

In fact, I was born to a Greek woman who was pregnant with me on her arrival in Melbourne and who married a newly-arrived Greek man later in the year I was born. They returned to Greece in the 1970s with their two sons, who were both born in Melbourne.

Meanwhile, my identity was swapped with that of another baby girl born on the same day in the same hospital as me. It's unknown whether this identity swap was accidental or deliberate— the hospital's destruction of relevant records in 1987 means I'll probably never know.

The other baby was placed with her adoptive family, also directly from the hospital, six days before I was placed with Dad and Mum. Forensic DNA testing facilitated by the AIS has confirmed her true identity as the biological daughter of the mother identified in my adoption and original birth records.

I've been actively seeking information about my background for well over 30 years now—since 1989 (when Bruce and I got married), and I began seeking contact with my biological kin in 1997 (the year that our twins, Hayley and Liam, were born too prematurely and passed away). Over that time, it's become more and more important to me to be able *to incorporate my biological and cultural heritage in my official identity*.

As I said earlier, this celebration is for something *quite unusual*. That's because there are only a handful of adoption discharges in Victoria each year, and most of them are on the grounds of complete breakdown in the social relationships between the adopted person and their adoptive family. However, my application was *not* for that reason—my application was based on the special circumstances associated with my misidentification.

I've been told repeatedly that mine is the *first time* a case of misidentification in an adoption has had to be dealt with by the Victorian authorities. I very much doubt that it will be the last …

3. Regardless, what do all these County Court orders mean going forward?

Well, the discharge of my Adoption Order means that the legal effect of that Adoption Order has been undone—so:

- my Adoption Order has ceased to be in force,
- I'm officially no longer an adopted person,
- I'm no longer legally connected to the Mackieson family, and
- I'm now legally reconnected to my original family.

The discharge of my Adoption Order *does not mean*, however, that my history with my adoptive family has been officially erased; that I no longer love my adoptive family members; or that my social relationships with my adoptive family will necessarily change (cross fingers):

- As I see it, I was socially adopted by Dad and Mum when I was *placed* with them at three weeks of age, even though my *legal* Adoption Order was not granted for another 14 months.
- The *legal* adoptive relationships have now ended but my *social* adoptive relationships with the Mackieson family continue—as evidenced, I trust, by the presence of several Mackieson family members here today (Unfortunately, due to numbers, we couldn't invite everyone).

The discharge of my Adoption Order also *does not mean* that I'll necessarily have a social relationship with my Greek mother, whose identity is now accurately recorded on my Birth Certificate. Indeed, to date she has consistently expressed that she wants *no* contact with me, either directly or through third parties on my behalf. I feel obliged, albeit reluctantly, to respect her wishes.

Regardless of that, and despite having missed the opportunity to know about it growing up, I'm proud of my Greek heritage. I'm also proud to reclaim my original name, *xxx Zagarelou*—which was apparently also the name of my maternal grandmother. This name—which apparently means "the light / light"—was a gift from my mother; a gift I'll always treasure, not only because it reflects Greek tradition in the naming of daughters. But also because, in the context of forced separation at birth and closed adoption practices, my mother could so easily *not* have given me a name at all.

According to a recent article by Gillian Bouras, an Australian author who married a Greek man and for most of her married life has resided in ✳✳✳ ✳✳✳✳✳ ✳✳✳✳✳✳✳✳ (where my mother still lives), to this day, Greek parents refer to their infant as "Baby" until *after* the ceremony of baptism. That would've posed an interesting challenge, wouldn't it? Would I have been so keen to change my name to *Penny Baby Zagarelou-Mackieson*? Maybe, Baby?

Implementation of the orders granted by the County Court *means that I now have new legal identity documents*—including birth certificate, driver's licence and passport.

I'm very excited that my upcoming maiden trip to Greece will be on my new passport under my new integrated name— something I never imagined in 2020 when we first planned this trip. Mind you, I also never imagined I'd ever seek the discharge of my Adoption Order.

Thanks

In the context of adoption, I believe the concept of kin is both fluid and inclusive. So, it has saddened me that there have been some casualties in my relationships with kin as a result of discovering I was swapped at birth—my wrongly identified maternal kin, with whom I was in false reunion for two decades, have discontinued contact with me.

On the other hand, I'm very glad that so many people in my kinship and friendship networks have stood by me—even if they haven't necessarily understood me—throughout this unexpected and strange period of my life. I truly appreciate and love you all.

I'd like to take this opportunity to thank a few people, in particular, who are in attendance today:

- Pauline Ley—Thank you for suggesting that I take an AncestryDNA test as a last resort to connect with my (then-believed-to-be putative) father's family and hopefully find a face that looks like mine. It's turned out very differently to what we imagined, but no one could empathise with my situation more than you. I now know the truth, at least some of it, and that is gold!

- Charlotte Smith, Manager of VANISH—Thank you for your support on so many levels. You've helped me navigate some extreme unintended consequences of forced and closed adoption practices at the same time as effectively engaging VANISH in a Parliamentary Inquiry concerning Historical Forced Adoption in Victoria, which we didn't anticipate either.

- To all my fabulous girlfriends (I won't name you individually—you know who you are)—Thank you for the countless deep and meaningful conversations—some even over the phone or coffee, not only wine and tears—that have helped me process each twist and turn and up and down of the roller coaster.

- To the two most significant men in my life: Bruce Minahan, my awesome partner, and Patrick Minahan, our wonderful son—who I'm fortunate has inherited from his mother not only his devotion to Melbourne Football Club, but also his 37% Greek DNA!

- Bruce—Thank you, especially for your encouragement to address my identity issues, and for so exuberantly embracing Paddy's and my newfound Greek heritage in our daily lives ... Though perhaps you could cut down on the Greek pastry purchases now—these kilos get harder to lose every year!

- Paddy—Thank you for so assertively keeping me grounded. You're absolutely right: not everything in life revolves around adoption.

- In anticipation, I also thank Bruce and Paddy, *and* my good friends Catherine Neville, Veronica Sakell and Bruce Gemmell (who from now on I'll be calling "the three ells") for joining me on my first trip to Greece. Όπα!

- Finally, Ευχαριστώ πολύ! Thank you very much—for your support in my surreal identity odyssey, and for joining us for this celebration today.

Now, please resume eating, drinking and chatting …

Απολαμβάνω! Enjoy!

APPENDIX III

Letter to Monash Health Board seeking apology, September 2022

Dr Penny Zagarelou-Mackieson

15 September 2022

The Chair and Directors of the Monash Health Board
Monash Medical Centre
246 Clayton Road
Clayton, VIC 3168

Dear Mr Sanghvi and fellow Directors,

Seeking a personal apology for historical wrongs

I write to request a personal apology from Monash Health for wrongs done to me at the Queen Victoria Memorial Hospital (QVMH) in 1963. Namely, QVMH staff separated me from my mother in coercive circumstances for the purpose of adoption ('forced adoption') and misidentified me (that is, swapped me with another baby) prior to my adoptive placement at three weeks of age.

Evidence

DNA test results show that I am not genetically related to the mother officially identified in my County Court of Victoria adoption records of 1964, and that that mother is the genetic mother of the person who was swapped with me at the QVMH (as identified by the Department of Justice and Community Safety's Adoption Services in 2019).

County Court of Victoria adoption records of 1963 relating to the person swapped with me indicate that a QVMH social worker placed her with her adoptive parents in a private adoption arrangement on   March 1963, but my mother's written consent was not obtained until the following day. This shows that QVMH gave my mother no choice but to relinquish her baby for adoption.

Based on legal advice from the Victorian Government Solicitor's Office (via the Department of Justice and Community Safety) and privately engaged solicitors, I pursued the only avenue available to me to correct the genealogical information recorded about me in Victoria's Birth and Adoption Registers and to legally integrate my true original identity. This involved applying to the County Court of Victoria to discharge my Adoption Order; correctly recognise me as the person born to the 'official' mother of the person swapped with me; make a legal name change that reflects my true identity; and issue a new birth certificate accordingly. I lodged my application on 13 August 2021 and it was successfully resolved on 15 March 2022, meaning that the presiding County Court Judge accepted the DNA evidence that I was swapped and misidentified at the QVMH prior to my adoptive placement.

Context

I have faced lifelong challenges associated with my adoption, about which I have always known but would never have chosen for myself. The recent discovery of my misidentification has added further trauma and complication and caused significant disruption to my life.

Nevertheless, I emphasise that I am not seeking financial compensation from Monash Health; rather, I am solely seeking a personal apology to facilitate my healing. I am aware that a public apology was

1

made in 2013 by Monash Health's Chief Executive to women who were forced to give up their babies at the QVMH up until the late 1970s. However, that apology does not adequately address the wrongs and harms done to the babies who were forcibly separated from their mothers and adopted, let alone the additional wrong done specifically to me and the subsequent harms inflicted through having also been misidentified.

Previous requests to Monash Health

This is the third time I have requested a personal apology from Monash Health. The first occasion was via letter sent in September 2021 to the Chief Executive by Macpherson Kelley solicitors on my behalf, and the second was via personal outreach to the Chief Executive in June 2022 by a former colleague who generously volunteered to advocate for me.

Destruction of QVMH records

Both previous requests also sought apology for wrongful destruction of my mother's and my QVMH records. Monash Health has advised that those records were likely destroyed when the QVMH and Monash Health merged in 1987, yet I understand that others born at the QVMH and subsequently adopted around the same time as I have gained access to their QVMH records. However, as a gesture of good faith, I have decided not to further pursue this particular matter.

Conclusion

I reiterate that I am seeking a personal apology from Monash Health. I expect the apology to be formal, written and genuine; and to acknowledge full and unconditional responsibility and offer deep regret for:

- QVMH staff having coercively separated me from my mother after my birth for the purpose of adoption;
- QVMH staff having misidentified me; and
- the harms inflicted on me as a result of those wrongs.

To progress the apology, I am willing to meet with appropriate representatives of Monash Health. At that time, if required, I can provide copies of the documents associated with my recent County Court of Victoria application that outline the evidence relating to the matters here raised.

I look forward to hearing from you at your earliest convenience.

Your sincerely,

Dr Penny Zagarelou-Mackieson
BSW, MSW, PhD *Melb*

2

185

APPENDIX IV

Letter of apology from Monash Health, 8 November 2022

Monash Health

Executive Office:
Monash Medical Centre
246 Clayton Road
Clayton Victoria 3168
Australia

Postal address:
Locked Bag 29
Clayton South Vic 3169
Australia

Tel (03) 9594 2738
Fax (03) 9594 6990

8 November 2022

Dr Penny Zagarelou-Mackieson

Dear Dr Zagarelou-Mackieson

I refer to your letter dated 15 September 2022, addressed to the Chair and Directors of the Monash Health Board, to which I am writing in reply, and to your previous correspondence.

As you are aware, Monash Health is legal successor to Queen Victoria Hospital. I would like to express my deepest regret for the events described in the Department of Justice and Community Safety report, which have resulted in you being placed for adoption in circumstances where your natural mother was incorrectly identified as

On behalf of Queen Victoria Hospital, I would like to sincerely apologise for the impact that this has had upon you, and the distress that this has caused when these circumstances became known to you.

I sincerely hope that this apology can facilitate healing, as you expressed in your letter, and wish you the very best for the future.

Yours sincerely

Professor Andrew Stripp
Chief Executive

Monash Medical Centre Clayton	Moorabbin Hospital	Kingston Centre	Dandenong Hospital	Casey Hospital	Community-based services across the South East
246 Clayton Road Clayton Tel: 9594 6666	Centre Road East Bentleigh Tel: 9928 8111	Warrigal Road Cheltenham Tel: 9265 1000	David Street Dandenong Tel: 9554 1000	Kangan Drive Berwick Tel: 8768 1200	ABN 82 142 080 338

APPENDIX V

Speech at VANISH AGM, 18 November 2022

From Adoption Deception to Donor Conception

There are many lessons from pre-1980s adoptions that we could reasonably expect Australian governments to have embedded in current policy, law and practice concerning adoption and donor conception. But they haven't.

This is a big topic for a panel to cover in 40 minutes, so I've decided to focus on only two of the many relevant and inter-related issues. Namely:

- Lack of priority on the rights of the child in general and, in particular,
- Ongoing failure to protect the child's right to their original/ natural identity.

But before diving in, I echo Simon and Charlotte's acknowledgements of the Traditional Owners of the land on which we meet, and also pay my respects.

Lack of priority on the rights of the child

Children's rights are part of the broader context of human rights, focusing on the vulnerable stage prior to adulthood in the continuum of human life.

The United Nations Convention on the Rights of the Child ('the Convention') is the primary international children's rights instrument. Introduced in 1989, it integrates all human rights concerning children.

This Convention is the most widely adopted international human rights instrument, the most rapidly ratified, and the quickest to have come into force. Every United Nations member state has ratified it, with the notable exception of the USA.

In the USA, the language of children's rights is used almost exclusively in relation to foster care and adoption.

Yet, the Convention does not suggest, implicitly or explicitly, that children have a right to be adopted if they can't be raised by their parents.

Nevertheless, adoption and adoptees are of particular interest in the Convention:

> Adoption is first mentioned in **Article 20** as one of a range of potential alternative care options for children identified by child protection authorities as unable to be safely cared for by their parents.
>
> **Article 21** also refers to adoption. But rather than encourage its use, Article 21 provides strong guidance concerned to restrict the use of adoption; to ensure implementation only by competent authorised bodies; and to require informed parental consent in most circumstances of child adoption. Article 21 also asserts that the *best interests* of the child should be the *paramount*, rather than a *primary*, consideration in matters pertaining to adoption.
>
> So, far from resoundingly advocating adoption, **Article 21** cautions governments about their use of adoption, which is unsurprising given the expectations of Western adoption and adoption services provision create tension with respect to other children's rights enshrined in the Convention.

Indeed, the Victorian Government was highly aware of those tensions in the 1980s during the decade-long process to formulate and introduce the Convention. During that time, the Victorian Government passed two important pieces of legislation that reflect an increased commitment to the rights of children in decision-making about their welfare. These are:

1. The then ground-breaking *Adoption Act 1984*, enabling adopted individuals to access their previously closed records. This remains Victoria's principal adoption legislation; and

2. The *Children & Young Persons Act 1989*, which introduced Permanent Care Orders as the preferred alternative to adoption of children from out-of-home care.

I emphasise that *there is no right to adopt a child* enshrined in any international instrument, despite that many intending parents wrongly assume it is inherent in their right to marry and found a family, as outlined in Article 16 of the Universal Declaration of Human Rights.

As a human rights instrument, the UN Convention on the Rights of the Child obliges party governments to respect and promote—that is, implement—EACH AND EVERY ONE of the principles and articles enshrined in it.

Party governments cannot pick and choose which principles and human rights they will implement because all rights are considered *equal*, as well as *mutually inter-related* and *inter-dependent* (or, in Convention language, "indivisible and interconnected").

Further, individuals cannot give up their rights, and their rights cannot be removed from them or bestowed on them as a gift or reward, even where those rights have been ignored or breached by the government or another organisation.

Ratification of the Convention thus involves an expectation that the country will implement ALL of the children's rights contained within the instrument EQUALLY.

The Australian Government ratified the Convention in 1990.

However, in the 32 years since, the Convention has not been incorporated in any specific laws enacted by the Australian Government, and its translation into relevant state and territory laws has been neither straightforward, consistent or complete.

In Victoria, for example, negligible real progress has been made since the 1980s that would indicate an operationalised commitment to a child rights approach to children's welfare.

Indeed, the evidence from my PhD research suggests that the Victorian Government has been **reversing** its commitment of the 1980s to strive for a child rights approach.

Numerous legal experts have also found that there "has been no direct incorporation of [the Convention] into the provisions of Victoria's child welfare legislation". For example:

> Neither the *Adoption Act 1984* or Victoria's current primary child protection legislation, the *Children, Youth and Families Act 2005*, require that decisions concerning the lives of children be made in accordance with their rights.
>
> Instead, those Acts rely on the *best interests* principle, even though it is only one of the four primary principles underpinning the Convention.

In other words, children continue to be treated as *objects* of international human rights law, not as *subjects* of human rights.

Little wonder that adopted and donor conceived children are denied equal protection under Victorian law, and that this discrimination extends into adulthood.

In my own case: As an individual in her late 50s who was adopted as a newborn infant, I recently had to apply to the County Court of Victoria (under provisions of the *Adoption Act 1984*) as the "adopted child", and the Court's decisions were based on being "satisfied that the welfare and interests of the child would be promoted".

This is beyond paternalistic—it's also infantilising, devaluing and demeaning, not to mention infuriating!

Numerous articles of the Convention apply to donor conception as well as to adoption

A child's right to *continuity of family connections* with their natural/biological parents, and by implication also with their siblings and extended family, is embodied in articles 7, 9 and 10:

Article 7 requires that a child be registered immediately after birth and have the rights to a name; to acquire a nationality; and to know and be cared for by their parents (meaning their natural/biological parents) *as far as possible.*

Article 9 dictates that a child should not be involuntarily separated from their parents, except where determined by competent authorities under judicial review to ensure the child's *best interests*; and that a child separated from their parent(s) be permitted to maintain their relationship(s) and contact with their parent(s), except where determined as being contrary to the child's *best interests.*

Article 10 states that a child has the right to maintain their relationships and contact with both parents where their parents reside in different jurisdictions.

A child's right to *continuity of culture* is embodied in articles 20, 29 and 30 (which I won't go through now); and a child's right to *continuity of identity* is embodied in Article 7 (which I mentioned earlier), as well as articles 8 and 29.

Article 8 obliges governments to respect the child's right to *legal preservation* of their identity, "including nationality, name and family relations"; and to quickly re-establish a child's identity where the child has suffered illegal deprivation of one or more elements of their identity.

Ongoing failure to protect the child's right to their original/natural identity

Article 8 is clearly NOT embedded in Victorian Government policy, law or practice. This is evident in the unequal treatment of birth certificates, despite:

- Numerous reviews of the key legislation in which adopted and donor conceived people have repeatedly raised the accuracy of their birth certificate as a critical issue for them; and

- Numerous amendments to the key legislation concerning adoption and donor conception since the Australian Government ratified the Convention in 1990.

In regard to adoption

If an Adoption Order was granted in the County Court next week for a locally-born child, the child's relationships with their family of origin and their original birth certificate would be legally cancelled; and a new post-adoption birth certificate would be issued recording their adoptive parents as if the child was born to them.

This is outlined in a Practice Note on the County Court's Adoption and Parentage List webpage, which states:

> The effect of the adoption will be that the details of the biological parent(s) will be removed and replaced by the details of the adoptive parent(s).

To put this into context, exactly the same thing happened when the County Court granted my Adoption Order nearly 60 years ago.

As I've learned the hard way, there is also no mechanism in Victoria by which an adopted person can readily re-establish their true original/natural identity if illegally deprived of it.

I recently discovered that I was misidentified before being placed for adoption at three weeks of age. I sought several legal opinions and all agreed that the only option available to legally re-establish and integrate my true original identity was to seek Discharge of my Adoption Order and recognition of my true original identity through the County Court.

My application took six months to resolve from the date of lodgement, and followed an earlier application to the County Court to obtain identifying information about my real natural mother, thus also about my real original identity, which took seven months to resolve.

Meanwhile, the Victorian Government's official legal position was that my Adoption Order remained valid. So, even if an integrated birth certificate was available to me, it would have wrongly identified both me and my natural mother, had I not applied to Discharge my Adoption Order.

In regard to donor conception

If a baby conceived by a donor treatment procedure through an Assisted Reproductive Technology (ART) clinic was born in Victoria next week, BDM would record "donor conceived" on the child's Birth Register entry and attach an addendum to their birth certificate stating that further information is available to the individual about the entry.

But this would happen only if the child's parent(s) advise BDM on the birth registration form, and/or if the respective ART provider advises VARTA which would then advise BDM.

Nevertheless, should VARTA or the individual concerned become aware of more, or more accurate, information at a later time, the *Assisted Reproductive Treatment Act 2008* provides for the correction or amendment of the details recorded on the Register via an administrative, rather than legal, process.

Alternatively, if a baby conceived by self-insemination was born in Victoria next week, the donor details cannot be recorded on the Central Register maintained by VARTA, nor will an addendum indicating further information be recorded by BDM and attached to the child's birth certificate.

This further discriminates against donor conceived people born outside the ART clinic system, as they have less access to information about their paternal identity through BDM than other donor conceived people born in Victoria.

Conclusion

The lack of focus by Australian governments on children's rights continues to *passively*, but effectively, elevate the interests of intending parents in adoption and donor conception policy, law and practice.

There hasn't been time to discuss it in this presentation, but it is also evident that Australian governments—including the Victorian Government—continue to *actively promote* the interests of intending parents over the rights of children. They do this through supporting the medicalisation of infertility, and championing particular LGBTIQ+ agendas in relation to having children. Despite the *progressive* rhetoric around individual choice and inclusiveness, current policy, law and practice in these areas is both *deceptive* and *regressive* in terms of children's rights, and serves to fuel the same market in babies that drove past appalling adoption and donor conception practices.

In conclusion, I believe that far too few lessons have been learned and implemented by Australian governments in relation to upholding the human rights of children and adults who are adopted or born of donor conception.

BIBLIOGRAPHY

3AW Afternoons with Dee Dee. (18 March 2022). 'Friday Lunch with Dee Dee and Grubby, March 18 (2022)'. (From 1:16:45 pm to 1:31:62 pm). <https://omny.fm/shows/afternoons-with-dee-dee/friday-lunch-w-ith-dee-dee-and-grubby-march-18-202>.

3CR 855am Community Radio. (29 September 2016). 'Penny Mackieson—Adoption'. <https://www.3cr.org.au/search/node/penny%20mackieson>.

3CR 855am Community Radio. (6 October 2016). 'Penny Mackieson—Permanent Care'. <https://www.3cr.org.au/search/node/penny%20mackieson>.

9 Entertainment. (2022). 'The 5 Most Heartbreaking Moments from Love Child'. <https://www.nine.com.au/entertainment/latest/love-child-tv-show-most-heartbreaking-moments/13248947-678e-481e-986f-c6a6d142fc71>.

Access Canberra. (2021). 'Integrated Birth Certificate Factsheet'. Canberra: ACT Government. <https://files.accesscanberra.act.gov.au/files/apply-for-a-birth-death-or-marriage-certificate/factsheet-integrated-birth-certificate-factsheet.pdf>.

Adams, Paul L. and Ivan Fras. (1988). *Beginning Child Psychiatry*. London and New York: Brunner-Routledge.

Adoption Act 1984 (Vic). 'Victorian Legislation'. Melbourne: Victorian Government. <https://www.legislation.vic.gov.au/in-force/acts/adoption-act-1984/073>.

Adoption of Children Act 1964 (Vic). <https://aiatsis.gov.au/sites/default/files/docs/digitised_collections/remove/53525.pdf> and <https://aiatsis.gov.au/sites/default/files/docs/digitised_collections/remove/53526.pdf>.

Albom, Mitch, quoted by Andi Willis. (2022). 'Inspiring Quotes About Family and Family History'. Good Life Photo Solutions. <https://goodlifephotosolutions.com/quotes-family-family-history/>.

Andrews, Daniel. (23 February 2015). 'Same-Sex Adoption A Step Closer With Review Of Laws' (Media Release). Melbourne: Premier of Victoria.

Andrews, Daniel and Colin Brooks. (12 October 2022). 'Past Care Leavers: We Hear You' (Media Release). Melbourne: Premier of Victoria.

Andrews, Daniel and Jaclyn Symes. (10 March 2022). 'Healing The Harm Of Forced Adoption' (Media Release). Melbourne: Premier of Victoria.

ARMS. (28 October 2018). 'Unveiling of the Memorial Statue in Melbourne 26 October 2018'. <https://www.armsvic.org.au/blog/unveiling-of-the-memorial-statue-in-melbourne-26th-october-2018>.

Arnaoutoglou, Ilias. (1998). *Ancient Greek Laws: A Sourcebook*. London and New York: Routledge.

Artemis Media. (2022). *Every Family Has A Secret*. <http://www.artemisfilms.com/productions/every-family-has-a-secret/>.

Australian Associated Press. (15 March 2022). '"I Never Felt Right": DNA Test Reveals Melbourne Woman Introduced to Wrong 'Biological Mother'. *The Guardian*. <https://www.theguardian.com/australia-news/2022/mar/15/i-never-felt-right-dna-test-reveals-melbourne-woman-introduced-to-wrong-biological-mother>.

Australian Bureau of Statistics. (2021). 'Births, Australia'. <https://www.abs.gov.au/statistics/people/population/births-australia/2021>.

Australian Institute of Health and Welfare. (2015, 2016, 2017, 2018, 2019, 2021a, 2021b, 2023). *Adoptions Australia*. Canberra: AIHW. <https://www.aihw.gov.au/reports-data/health-welfare-services/adoptions/reports>.

Australian Institute of Health and Welfare. (2017). *Adoptions Australia 2016–17*, Appendices. A and B. Canberra: AIHW. <https://www.aihw.gov.au/getmedia/c54bf6ea-00f1-4e7f-a203-4103b8efa10a/aihw-cws-61-appendixes-a-b.pdf.aspx>.

Australian Institute of Health and Welfare. (2021). 'Adoptions, Glossary'. Canberra: AIHW. <https://www.aihw.gov.au/reports-data/health-welfare-services/adoptions/glossary>.

Australian Institute of Health and Welfare. (2018). *Child Protection Australia 2016–17*. Canberra: AIHW. <https://www.aihw.gov.au/reports/child-protection/child-protection-australia-2016-17/contents/summary>.

Australian Institute of Health and Welfare. (2021). *Child Protection Australia 2019–20*. Canberra: AIHW. <https://www.aihw.gov.au/reports/child-protection/child-protection-australia-2019-20/summary>.

Baden, Amanda. (2016). '"Do You Know Your *Real* Parents?" and Other Adoption Microaggressions'. *Adoption Quarterly*, 19 (1). <https://doi.org/10.1080/10926755.2015.1026012>.

The Bairnsdale Advertiser. (31 March 1980). 'Closure of Buchan South Exchange', pp. 6–7.

Bell, Jessica. (2020). 'Adoption Discovery: 59-year-old Man Finds Secret Family'. *7news.com.au.* <https://7news.com.au/lifestyle/parenting/59-year-old-man-discovers-he-has-a-secret-family-c-712982>.

The Big Australia Bucket List. (2022). 'Timeline of Every Victoria Lockdown (Dates and Restrictions)'. <https://bigaustraliabucketlist.com/victoria-lockdowns-dates-restrictions/>.

Births, Deaths and Marriages Registration Act 1996 (Vic). 'Victorian Legislation'. Melbourne: Victorian Government. <https://www.legislation.vic.gov.au/in-force/acts/births-deaths-and-marriages-registration-act-1996/040>.

Blythe, Stacy and Karleen Gribble. (2019). *Belonging in Two Families: Exploring Permanency Options for Children in Long-Term Out-of-Home Care in Australia.* NSW: Adopt Change and Western Sydney University.

Buckley, Gail L., quoted by Andi Willis. (2020). 'Inspiring Quotes About Family and Family History'. Good Life Photo Solutions. <https://goodlifephotosolutions.com/quotes-family-family-history/>.

BrainyQuote. (2001–2022). 'Daniel Patrick Moynihan Quotes'. <https://www.brainyquote.com/quotes/daniel_patrick_moynihan_182347>.

Bretherton, Tanya, Karleen Gribble and Renee Carter. (2017). *Barriers to Adoption in Australia.* Surry Hills, NSW: Adopt Change.

Britannica. (2023). 'DNA Chemical Compound'. <https://www.britannica.com/science/DNA>.

Bryony. (2 June 2016). 'The DNA Journey: Powered by AncestryDNA'. Ancestry Corporate. <https://www.ancestry.com/corporate/blog/the-dna-journey-powered-by-ancestrydna>.

Centre of Excellence. (2 September 2022). 'Why Greek Mythology is Still Relevant'. <https://www.centreofexcellence.com/greek-mythology-still-relevant/>.

Children's Court of Victoria. (2022). Annual Report 2021–22. Melbourne: Children's Court of Victoria. <ChildrensCourtVIC_Annual Report 2021-22.pdf>.

Coalition Internationale pour l'Abolition de la Maternité de Substitution (CIAMS). <http://abolition-ms.org/en/home/>.

Chalek, Mike and Jessica Gardner. (2012). *Fraud on the Court: One Adoptee's Fight to Reclaim His Identity.* USA: Universal Technical Systems.

Collins Dictionary. (2022). 'Definition of "Unadopted"'. <https://www.collinsdictionary.com/dictionary/english/unadopted>.

Commission for Children and Young People. (2017). *Safe and Wanted: Inquiry Into the Implementation of the Children, Youth and Families Amendment (Permanent Care and Other Matters) Act 2014.* Melbourne: CCYP.

Communities and Justice. (2022). 'Introducing Integrated Birth Certificates'. NSW: NSW Government. <https://www.facs.nsw.gov.au/families/adoption/introducing-integrated-birth-certificates>.

Conn, Peter J. (2013). *Adoption: A Brief Social and Cultural History.* Basingstoke: Palgrave Macmillan.

Cooper, Adam. (18 July 2011). 'Switch Shock As Newborns Go To Wrong Families'. *The Age.*

County Court of Victoria. (2022). 'Adoption and Parentage'. <https://www.countycourt.vic.gov.au/going-court/adoption-and-parentage>.

Crane, Tara R. (2000). 'Mistaken Baby Switches: An Analysis of Hospital Liability and Resulting Custody Issues'. *Journal of Legal Medicine,* 21 (1), pp. 109–124.

Daley, Katerina. (9 August 2022). 'My Big Fat Greek Wedding: 10 Most Iconic Quotes'. *ScreenRant.* <https://screenrant.com/my-big-fat-greek-wedding-best-quotes/>.

Deery, Shannon. (22 October 2022). 'State's Integrity Deficit: Watchdog Warns on "Soft Corruption"'. *Herald Sun.*

Department of Economic and Social Affairs, Population Division. (2009). *Child Adoption: Trends and Policies.* New York: United Nations.

Department of Health. (2022). 'Public Fertility Care Services'. Victoria: Victorian Government. <https://www.health.vic.gov.au/public-health/public-fertility-care-services>.

Department of Justice and Community Safety. (2022). 'Discharge of Adoption'. Melbourne: Victoria State Government. <https://www.justice.vic.gov.au/your-rights/adoption/discharge-of-adoption>.

Department of Social Services. (29 March 2023). 'Tenth Anniversary of the National Apology for Forced Adoptions, 21 March 2013'. Canberra: Australian Government. <https://www.dss.gov.au/families-and-children-programs-services-family-relationships-forced-adoption-practices/national-apology-for-forced-adoptions-10th-anniversary-transcript-0>.

Dexter, Rachael, Paul Sakkal and Simone F. Koob. (24 July 2020). '"Stressing Me Out Beyond Belief": Government Clarifies Advice on Maternity Visits'. *The Age.*

Devillers, Marie-Josèphe and Ana-Luana Stoicea-Deram. (Eds). (2021). *Towards the Abolition of Surrogate Motherhood.* Mission Beach: Spinifex Press.

DNA Down Under. (23 August 2019). 'Melbourne'. <https://www.dnadownunder.com/melbourne/>.

Donor Conceived Australia. (2022). <https://www.facebook.com/DonorConceivedAustralia/?ref=page_internal>.

Ekis Ekman, Kajsa. (2013). *Being and Being Bought: Prostitution, Surrogacy and the Split Self.* North Melbourne: Spinifex Press.

Faculty of Medicine, Dentistry and Health Sciences. (2022). 'Nursing: Dr Madonna Grehan'. Melbourne: The University of Melbourne. <https://mdhs. unimelb.edu.au/engage/alumni/alumni/alumni-profiles/health-sciences/ nursing/nursing-dr-madonna-grehan>.

Families, Fairness and Housing. (2022) 'Adoption Victoria'. Melbourne: Victoria State Government. <https://services.dffh.vic.gov.au/adoption-victoria#:~:text=On%201%20July%202019%2C%20delivery,Local%20 adoption>.

Families, Fairness and Housing. (2022). 'Families and Children: Foster Care'. Melbourne: Victoria State Government. <https://services.dffh.vic.gov.au/ foster-care>.

Flanagan, Martin. (20 September 2021). 'Penny Mackieson'. *The Age*.

Foley, Martin. (6 October 2015). 'Adoption Equality For Children Of Same-Sex Couples' (Media Release). Melbourne: Premier of Victoria.

Foley, Martin. (12 May 2021). 'Public IVF To Make Starting A Family Easier For Victorians' (Media Release). Melbourne: Victoria State Government.

Gibbons, Ann. (2 August 2017). 'The Greeks Really Do Have Near-Mythical Origins, Ancient DNA Reveals'. *Science*.

Gittins, Ross. (30 September 2020). 'If You Do Health Admin On The Cheap, Don't Be Amazed If Things Go Wrong'. *The Age*.

Government of South Australia. (2022). 'Change to the Adoption Act'. <https:// www.childprotection.sa.gov.au/adoption/changes-to-the-adoption-act>.

The Greek Herald. (30 April 2021). 'What is the Custom of Protomagia (1 May) and Why Do Greeks Celebrate It?'. <https://greekherald.com.au/culture/what-is-the-custom-of-protomagia-1st-of-may-and-why-do-greeks-celebrate-i/#:~:text=It%20was%20named%20after%20the,the%20good%20and%20 the%20bad>.

The Greens ACT. (23 July 2020). 'Recognising the Lived Experience of Canberrans in Birth Documents'. <https://greens.org.au/act/news/ recognising-lived-experience-canberrans-birth-documents>.

Gribble, Karleen. (2016). 'Submission to the Victorian Law Reform Commission's Review of the Adoption Act 1984' (Submission No. 59). <https://www. lawreform.vic.gov.au/wp-content/uploads/2021/09/Submission_CP_59_Dr_ Karleen_Gribble_28-09-16.pdf>.

Gribble, Karleen and Stacy Blythe. (28 November 2019). 'Adoption Law Should be Reformed to Give Children Legal Connections to Both of Their Families'. *The Conversation*.

Griffith, Keith C., quoted by Mirah Riben. (20 January 2015). 'Living With Adoption's Dichotomies and Myths'. *Huffington Post*.

Hennessy, Jill, Martin Foley and Jenny Mikakos. (18 June 2019). 'Fairer Birth Certificates For Trans And Gender Diverse Victorians' (Media Release). Melbourne: Premier of Victoria.

Hennessy, Jill and Martin Foley. (1 May 2020). 'Laws Commence To Deliver Fairer Birth Certificates' (Media Release). Melbourne: Premier of Victoria.

Hetherington, Toni. (14 May 2019). 'How Greek Mythology Continues to Have a Large Influence on Our Modern Lives'. *KidsNews*.

Higgins, Daryl and Sue Tait. (2015). *Request for Feedback and Input on Issues Paper: Establishing an Institute of Open Adoption*. Melbourne: Institute of Family Studies.

House of Representatives Standing Committee on Social Policy and Legal Affairs. (2018). *Breaking Barriers: A National Adoption Framework for Australian Children*. Canberra: The Parliament of the Commonwealth of Australia.

Huebner, Sabine R. (2013). 'Adoption and Fosterage in the Ancient Eastern Mediterranean'. *Childhood and Education in the Classical World*, pp. 510–531.

Hull, Crispin. (c. 2003). 'Chapter 7—Unusual and Interesting Cases From The High Court of Australia 1903–2003'. <http://www.crispinhull.com.au/high-court-book/chapter-seven-unusual-and-interesting-cases/>.

Iliadou, Maria. (2012). 'Supporting Women in Labour'. *Health Science Journal*, 6 (3), pp. 385–391.

Ilyushina, Mary. (16 May 2020). 'Dozens of Surrogacy Babies Stranded by Coronavirus Lockdown in Ukraine, Lawmaker Says'. *CNN*. <https://edition.cnn.com/2020/05/15/europe/ukraine-surrogacy-babies-lockdown-intl/index.html>.

International Foster Care Organisation. 'Dr Stacy Blythe (Australia)'. IFCO. <https://www.ifco.info/stacy-blythe-australia/>.

International Society of Genetic Genealogy Wiki. (2018). 'Timeline: History of Genetic Genealogy'. <https://isogg.org/wiki/Timeline:History_of_genetic_genealogy>.

Jackel, Laura. (3 February 2023). 'Everything We Know About the New Fertility TV Series Big Miracles'. *MamaMia*.

Jefford, Sarah. (2023). 'Sarah Jefford Awarded Medal of the Order of Australia'. <https://sarahjefford.com/sarah-jefford-order-of-australia/>.

Justice and Community Safety. (2022). 'Adopt a Child'. Melbourne: Victoria State Government. <https://www.justice.vic.gov.au/your-rights/adoption/adopt-a-child>.

Justice and Community Safety. (2022). 'Adoption'. Melbourne: Victoria State Government. <https://www.justice.vic.gov.au/your-rights/adoption>.

Justice and Community Safety (2022). 'Adoption Legislation, Standards and Resources'. Melbourne: Victoria State Government. <https://www.justice.vic. gov.au/your-rights/adoption/adoption-legislation-standards-and-resources>.

Justice and Community Safety. (2022). 'Forced Adoption Exceptional Circumstances Fund'. Melbourne: Victoria State Government. <https://www. justice.vic.gov.au/forced-adoption-hardship-fund>.

Katella, Kathy. (17 November 2022). 'Omicron, Delta, Alpha, and More: What To Know About the Coronavirus Variants'. *Yale Medicine*.

Kenny, Pauline, Daryl J. Higgins and Samuel R. Morley. (2015). *Good Practice Principles in Providing Services to Those Affected by Forced Adoption and Family Separation*. Melbourne: Australian Institute of Family Studies.

Klein, Renate. (2017). *Surrogacy: A Human Rights Violation*. Mission Beach: Spinifex Press.

Koman, Tess. (21 January 2016). '7 Babies Were Given to the Wrong Mothers in Australian Hospitals'. *Cosmopolitan*.

Lahl, Jennifer, Melinda Tankard Reist and Renate Klein. (Eds). (2019). *Broken Bonds: Surrogate Mothers Speak Out*. Mission Beach: Spinifex Press.

Lawrence, Carmen. (2006). *Fear and Politics*. Melbourne: Scribe Short Books.

Le Grand, Chip and Paul Sakkal. (5 November 2022). 'IBAC Probe Uncovers a Troubling Picture'. *The Age*.

Legislative Assembly Legal and Social Issues Standing Committee. (6 November 2019). 'Forced Adoptions Inquiry Launched' (Media Release). Melbourne: Parliament of Victoria.

Legislative Assembly Legal and Social Issues Committee. (2019). 'Terms of Reference: Inquiry into Responses to Historical Forced Adoptions in Victoria'. <https://www.parliament.vic.gov.au/images/stories/committees/lsic-LA/ Terms_of_Reference_-_adoption.pdf>.

Legislative Assembly Legal and Social Issues Committee. (2021). *Inquiry Into Responses to Historical Forced Adoptions in Victoria*. Melbourne: Parliament of Victoria. <https://www.parliament.vic.gov.au/images/stories/committees/ lsic-LA/Inquiry_into_Responses_to_Historical_Forced_Adoptions_in_ Victoria_/LALSIC_59-03_Responses_to_historical_forced_adoption_in_Vic. pdf>.

Lehmann, Claire. (10 February 2023). 'Acceptance, Not Surgery, Solution To Teen Trans Anxiety'. *The Australian*.

Lindsay, Hugh. (2009). *Adoption in the Roman World*. Cambridge: Cambridge University Press.

Lindsay, Hugh. (2010). 'Adoption and Heirship in Greece and Rome' in Beryl Rawson (Ed.). *A Companion to Families in the Greek and Roman*

Worlds. John Wiley and Sons. <https://onlinelibrary.wiley.com/doi/book/10.1002/9781444390766>.

Lunda, Petronellah, Catharina S. Minnie and Petronella Benadé. (2018). 'Women's Experiences of Continuous Support During Childbirth: A Meta-Synthesis'. *BMC Pregnancy and Childbirth*, 18 (167). <https://bmcpregnancychildbirth.biomedcentral.com/articles/10.1186/s12884-018-1755-8>.

Mackieson, Penny. (2015). *Adoption Deception: A Personal and Professional Journey*. North Melbourne: Spinifex Press.

Mackieson, Penny. (2016). 'How to Avoid Repeating Adoption Mistakes of Australia's Past'. *Children and Families in Focus*, March 2016 (2), pp. 77–80.

Mackieson, Penny. (4 October 2016). 'Adoption Laws Should Not Sever Biological Ties'. *Times-Spectator*, p. 11.

Mackieson, Penny. (20 October 2016). 'Birth Certificates: The Elephant in The Room in Gender and Adoption Debates'. *New Matilda*. <https://newmatilda.com/2016/10/20/birth-certificates-the-elephant-in-the-room-in-gender-and-adoption-debates/>.

Mackieson, Penny. (2017). 'Letter to the Editor: The Silencing of Lived Experience: The Author's Response to a Review of Adoption Deception'. *Children Australia*, 43 (1), pp. 88–89.

Mackieson, Penny. (2018). 'Submission to the House of Representatives Standing Committee on Social Policy and Legal Affairs National Inquiry into Local Adoption'. (Submission No. 61). <https://www.aph.gov.au/Parliamentary_Business/Committees/House/Social_Policy_and_Legal_Affairs/Localadoption/Submissions>.

Mackieson, Penny. (2019). The Introduction and Implementation of Permanent Care Orders in Victoria (PhD Thesis). Melbourne: Department of Social Work, Faculty of Medicine, Dentistry and Health Sciences, The University of Melbourne.

Mackieson, Penny. (10 December 2020). 'Adoption, Deception, and DNA Questions'. *Vanish Voice Summer 2020*, pp. 4–6 <https://vanish.org.au/news-events/newsletters/vanish-voice-summer-2020>.

Mackieson, Penny, Aron Shlonsky and Marie Connolly. (2017). 'Permanency Planning and Ideology in Western Child Welfare Systems: Implications for Victoria'. *Communities, Children and Families Australia*, 11 (1), pp. 3–16.

Mackieson, Penny, Aron Shlonsky and Marie Connolly. (2018). 'Informing Permanent Care Discourses: A Thematic Analysis of Parliamentary Debates in Victoria'. *The British Journal of Social Work*, 48 (8), pp. 2137–2156.

Mackieson, Penny, Aron Shlonsky and Marie Connolly. (2019). 'Increasing Rigor and Reducing Bias in Qualitative Research: A Document Analysis of Parliamentary Debates Using Applied Thematic Analysis'. *Qualitative Social Work,* 18 (6), pp. 865–980.

Mackieson, Penny, Aron Shlonsky and Marie Connolly. (2019). 'Permanent Care Orders in Victoria: A Thematic Analysis of Implementation Issues'. *Australian Social Work,* 72 (4), pp. 419–433.

Martin, Damon and Delphine Stadler. (2016). 'Promising Practice: Australia's National Apology for Forced Adoptions' in Christina Baglietto, Nigel Cantwell and Mia Dambach. (Eds). *Responding to Illegal Adoptions: A Professional Handbook.* Geneva. Switzerland: International Social Service.

McCubbing, Gus. (15 March 2022). 'Adoptee's 33-year Journey to 'Right' Name'. *The Ararat Advertiser.* <https://www.araratadvertiser.com.au/story/7659639/adoptees-33-year-journey-to-right-name/>.

McLysaght, Emer. (2011). 'Baby Mix-Up at Australian Hospital'. *thejournal.ie.* <https://www.thejournal.ie/baby-mix-up-at-australian-hospital-180009-Jul2011/>.

Melbourne School of Health Sciences. (11 November 2016). '2016 UMSWAA Dinner'. Melbourne: The University of Melbourne. <https://healthsciences.unimelb.edu.au/news-and-events/2016-umswaa-dinner>.

Mikakos, Jenny. (30 August 2016). 'Call to Comment on Outdated Adoption Laws' (Media Release). Melbourne: Department of Human Services, State Government of Victoria.

Mikakos, Jenny and Martin Pakula. (7 June 2017). 'Victorian Government Welcomes Adoption Review' (Media Release). Melbourne: Premier of Victoria.

Monash Health Historical Archives Collection. (Accessed 2023). 'Infants in the Queen Victoria Hospital Maternity Ward'.

News.com.au. (2015). '"Baby Sophie" Appeals for Parents to Come Forward, 17 Years After Being Dumped in a Public Toilet Block'. *news.com.au.*

O'Halloran, Kerry. (2021). *The Politics of Adoption: International Perspectives on Law, Policy and Practice* (Fourth Edition). Switzerland: Springer Nature Switzerland.

Overnights with Rod Quinn. (19 November 2016). 'Adoption in Australia'. ABC Radio. <https://www.abc.net.au/radio/programs/overnights/adoption-in-australia/8040222>.

Pakula, Martin and Martin Foley. (18 August 2016). 'Birth Certificates to Reflect True Identity' (Media Release). Melbourne: Premier of Victoria.

Parliament of Australia. (28 March 2018). 'New Review Into Barriers to Local Adoption' (Media Release). Canberra: Parliament of Australia.

Parliament of Australia. (2018). *Breaking Barriers: A National Adoption Framework for Australian Children (Report)*. <https://www.aph.gov.au/Parliamentary_Business/Committees/House/Social_Policy_and_Legal_Affairs/Localadoption/Report>.

Parliament of Australia. (2019). *Government Response: Breaking Barriers: A National Adoption Framework for Australian Children*. <https://www.aph.gov.au/Parliamentary_Business/Committees/House/Social_Policy_and_Legal_Affairs/Localadoption/Government_Response>.

Parliament of New South Wales. (2022). 'Adoption Legislation Amendment (Integrated Birth Certificates) Bill 2020'. <https://www.parliament.nsw.gov.au/bills/Pages/bill-details.aspx?pk=3771>.

Parliament of Victoria. (2021). 'Hearings and Transcripts, Inquiry into Responses to Historical Forced Adoptions in Victoria'. <https://www.parliament.vic.gov.au/lsic-la/article/4255>.

Parliament of Victoria. (2021). 'Report Tabled, Inquiry into Responses to Historical Forced Adoptions in Victoria'. <https://www.parliament.vic.gov.au/lsic-la/inquiry/973>.

Parliament of Victoria. (2022). 'Justice Legislation Amendment Bill 2022'. <https://content.legislation.vic.gov.au/sites/default/files/bills/591363bi1.pdf>.

Peraki, Martha and Catherine Vougiouklaki. (18 May 2015). 'How Has Greek Influenced the English Language?'. *British Council*. <www.britishcouncil.org>.

Porter, Christian. (29 October 2014). 'Adoption and Child Protection'. *Australian Polity*, 5 (1), pp. 15–25.

Ross, Anne. (2019). 'Taken Not Given—of Love and Loss'. <https://www.anneross.com.au/public-art-commissions-2/taken-not-given-of-love-and-loss>.

Quartly, Marian, Shurlee Swain and Denise Cuthbert. (2013). *The Market in Babies: Stories of Australian Adoption*. Clayton, Victoria: Monash University Publishing.

Queen Victoria Women's Centre. (2019). 'History of Queen Victoria Women's Centre'. <https://www.qvwc.org.au/history>.

Quirk, Christin. (2013). 'The Business of Adoption: Past Practices at Melbourne's Royal Women's Hospital'. *Lilith: A Feminist History Journal*, 19, pp. 46–58.

Regalado, Anthony. (12 February 2018). '2017 Was The Year Consumer DNA Testing Blew Up'. *MIT Technology Review*. <https://www.technologyreview.com/2018/02/12/145676/2017-was-the-year-consumer-dna-testing-blew-up/>.

Riley, Helen J. (2012). Identity and Genetic Origins: An Ethical Exploration of the Late Discovery of Adoptive and Donor-Insemination Offspring Status (Thesis). Queensland: Queensland University of Technology.

Rishworth, Amanda. (21 March 2023). 'Government Marks Ten Year Anniversary of the National Apology for Forced Adoptions' (Media Release). Canberra: Ministers for the Department of Social Services, Australian Government. <https://ministers.dss.gov.au/media-releases/10661>.

Robertson, James. (21 January 2016). 'NSW Health Confirms Seven Babies Given to Wrong Mothers in Mix-Up'. *The Sydney Morning Herald*.

Rubinstein, Lene. (1993). *Adoption in IV. Century Athens*. Copenhagen: Museum Tusculanum Press.

Sauer, Charles W. and Krishelle L. Marc-Aurele. (2016). 'Parent Misidentification Leading to the Breastfeeding of the Wrong Baby in a Neonatal Intensive Care Unit'. *The American Journal of Case Reports*, 17, pp. 574–579.

SBS. (2022). SBS On Demand: *Every Family Has A Secret*. <https://www.sbs.com. au/ondemand/tv-series/every-family-has-a-secret/season-1>.

SBS. (2020). *Who We Are*. <https://www.sbs.com.au/aboutus/who-we-are>.

SBS One. (2022). *The Surrogates*. <https://www.tvcatchupaustralia.com/the-surrogates>.

Senate Community Affairs References Committee (2012). *Commonwealth Contribution to Former Forced Adoption Policies and Practices*. Canberra: Commonwealth of Australia. <https://www.aph.gov.au/parliamentary_ business/committees/senate/community_affairs/completed_inquiries/ 2010-13/commcontribformerforcedadoption/report/index>.

Serry, Tanya, Tonya Stebbins, Andrew Martchenko, Natalie Araujo and Brigid McCarthy. (10 May 2022). 'Improving Access to COVID-19 Information by Ensuring the Readability of Government Websites'. *Health Promotion Journal of Australia*.

Shepherd, Tory. (6 February 2023) '"I Had Two Babies Born Last Week": The Unregulated World of Australia's Online Sperm Donors'. *The Guardian*. <https://www.theguardian.com/science/2023/feb/06/i-had-two-babies-born-last-week-the-unregulated-world-of-australias-online-sperm-donors>.

Simons, Margaret. (30 October 2022). 'The Daniel Andrews Paradox: The Enduring Appeal of Australia's Most Divisive Premier'. *The Guardian*. <https:// www.theguardian.com/australia-news/2022/oct/30/the-daniel-andrews-paradox-the-enduring-appeal-of-australias-most-divisive-premier>.

Standing Committee on Social Issues. (2000). *Releasing the Past: Adoption Practices 1950–1998, Final Report* (Parliamentary Paper No. 600). NSW: Legislative Council, NSW Parliament.

Stone, Kylie. (27 July 2020). 'Two-Hour Hospital Limit a Bitter Blow for Newborn Parents'. *The Age*.

Sukkar, Michael. (22 March 2023). 'Statement: National Apology for Forced Adoption—Tenth Anniversary'. Canberra: Michael Sukkar MP, Australian

Government. <https://www.michaelsukkar.com.au/speeches/statement-national-apology-for-forced-adoption-10th-anniversary/>.

Symes, Jaclyn. (5 April 2022). 'Helping Adopted Victorians Record Their Birth History' (Media Release). Melbourne: Premier of Victoria.

Theoi.com. (2017). 'Asklepios'. <https://www.theoi.com/Ouranios/Asklepios.html>.

Tomazin, Farah. (21 February 2015). 'Same-Sex Couples a Step Closer to Equal Adoption Rights in Victoria'. *The Age.* <https://www.theage.com.au/national/victoria/samesex-couples-a-step-closer-to-equal-adoption-rights-in-victoria-20150221-13kzib.html>.

Topsfield, Jewel. (27 December 2019). '"It Walks With You Forever": Mothers Sue Hospital That Took Their Babies'. *The Age.* <https://www.theage.com.au/national/victoria/it-walks-with-you-forever-mothers-sue-hospital-that-took-their-babies-20191227-p53n86.html>.

Tregeagle, Susan and Deirdre Cheers. (2016). 'Searching For Truths in the Debate About Adoption From Care'. *Children Australia,* 41 (3), pp. 240–242.

Tregeagle, Susan, Elizabeth Cox, Louise Voigt and Lynne Moggach. (2012). 'Are We Adequately Considering Children's Rights to a Family?: The Importance of Adoption to Young People in Long-Term Care'. *Developing Practice: The Child, Youth and Family Work Journal,* 31, pp. 62–69.

UNICEF. (1989). *United Nations Convention on the Rights of the Child.* Geneva, Switzerland: UNICEF. <https://www.unicef.org/child-rights-convention/convention-text>.

University of Melbourne Library. (2017). 'Winged Victory Coat of Arms, University of Melbourne'. Melbourne: The University of Melbourne. <https://digitised-collections.unimelb.edu.au/items/6445b66a-5e4f-5695-9bf9-5dd9f3bd6601>.

Van Steen, Gonda. (2019). *Adoption, Memory, and Cold War Greece: Kid Pro Quo?* Michigan, USA: University of Michigan Press.

Van Steen, Gonda. (2020). 'Professor Gonda Van Steen'. London, UK: King's College London. <https://www.kcl.ac.uk/people/gonda-van-steen>.

Van Steen, Gonda. (2023). 'Adoption's Unfinished Business' in Mary Cardaras (Ed.). *Voices of the Lost Children of Greece: Oral Histories of Cold War International Adoption.* UK and USA: Anthem Press.

VANISH Inc. (2016). 'Submission to the Victorian Law Reform Commission's Review of the Adoption Act 1984' (Submission No. 34). <https://www.lawreform.vic.gov.au/wp-content/uploads/2021/09/Submission_CP_34_VANISH_16-09-16.pdf>.

VANISH Inc. (2018). 'VANISH Founding Member Honoured in Queen's Birthday Awards'. *Voice* Winter 2018. <https://vanish.org.au/media/91688/voice-winter-2018.pdf>.

VANISH Inc. (2022). 'About VANISH'. <https://vanish.org.au/>.

Victorian Government. (2022). *Pride in Our Future: Victoria's LGBTIQ+ Strategy 2022–32.* Melbourne: Department of Families, Fairness and Housing, Victorian Government.

Victorian Government. (2022). *Victorian Government Response to the Recommendations of the Legislative Assembly Legal and Social Issues Committee's Inquiry into Responses to Historical Forced Adoptions in Victoria.* <https://www.parliament.vic.gov.au/file_uploads/Victorian_Government_Response_to_Inquiry_into_Responses_to_Historical_Forced_Adoptions_in_Victoria_j9vCQ6wr.pdf>.

Victorian Government. (2022). 'Victorian Legislation, Justice Legislation Amendment Bill 2022'. <https://www.legislation.vic.gov.au/bills/justice-legislation-amendment-bill-2022>.

Victorian Law Reform Commission. (2015). 'Adoption Act: Terms of Reference'. Melbourne: Victorian Law Reform Commission. <https://www.lawreform.vic.gov.au/publication/adoption-act-terms-of-reference/>.

Victorian Law Reform Commission. (2016). *Review of the Adoption Act 1984: Consultation Paper.* Melbourne: Victorian Law Reform Commission.

Victorian Law Reform Commission. (2017). *Review of the Adoption Act 1984: Report.* Melbourne: Victorian Law Reform Commission.

Victorian Legislation. (2015). 'Adoption Amendment (Adoption by Same-Sex Couples) Bill 2015'. <https://www.legislation.vic.gov.au/bills/adoption-amendment-adoption-same-sex-couples-bill-2015>.

Victorian Legislation. (2022). 'Births, Deaths and Marriages Registration Amendment Bill'. <https://www.legislation.vic.gov.au/bills/all-bills?page=1&sort%5B_score%5D=desc&sort%5Btitle_az%5D=asc&queryType=title_content&q=Births%2C+Deaths+and+Marriages+Bill>.

Victorian Legislation. (2022). 'Births, Deaths and Marriages Registration Amendment Bill 2019'. <https://www.legislation.vic.gov.au/bills/births-deaths-and-marriages-registration-amendment-bill-2019>.

Vité, Sylvain and Hervé Boéchat. (2008). *A Commentary on the United Nations Convention on the Rights of the Child, Article 21: Adoption.* <https://brill.com/display/title/11637>.

Wahlquist, Calla. (2 October 2021). 'How Melbourne's "Short, Sharp" Covid Lockdowns Became the Longest in the World'. *The Guardian.* <https://www.theguardian.com/australia-news/2021/oct/02/how-melbournes-short-sharp-covid-lockdowns-became-the-longest-in-the-world>.

Walsh, Hannah and Tegan Philpott. (18 December 2022). 'Surrogacy Is on the Increase in Australia, But Agreements Can Be Legally, Medically and Emotionally Complex'. *ABC News*. <https://www.abc.net.au/news/2022-12-18/surrogacy-increases-australia-complex-legally-emotionally/101664552>.

Wikipedia. (2022). 'Genealogical DNA Test'. <https://en.wikipedia.org/wiki/Genealogical_DNA_test>.

Wikipedia. (2022). 'Nike (Mythology)'. <https://en.wikipedia.org/wiki/Nike_(mythology)>.

Wikipedia. (2022). 'Penelope'. <https://en.wikipedia.org/wiki/Penelope>.

Wikipedia. (2022). 'Special Broadcasting Service'. <https://en.wikipedia.org/wiki/Special_Broadcasting_Service>.

World Health Organization. (2022). 'The WHO Logo and Emblem'. World Health Organization. <https://www.who.int/about/policies/publishing/logo>.

Yoffe, Jeanette. (2021). 'Genetic Mirroring: What It Is, How It Affects Adopted People, and What You Can Do About It'. *Jeanette-ically Speaking*. <https://www.youtube.com/watch?v=QMBS0ASF4Uo>.

Further Reading

Harms to babies and their mothers from separation after birth

Bergman, Nils J. (2014). 'The Neuroscience of Birth—and the Case for Zero Separation'. *Curationis*, 37. <https://curationis.org.za/index.php/curationis/article/view/1440/1453>.

Bergman, Nils J. (2019). 'Birth Practices: Maternal-Neonate Separation as a Source of Toxic Stress'. *Birth Defects Research*, 111 (15), pp. 1087–1109.

Bystrova, Ksenia, Valentina Ivanova, Maigun Edhborg, Ann-Sofi Matthieson, Anna-Berit Ransjö-Arvidson, Rifkat Mukhamedrakhimov (…). (2009). 'Early Contact Versus Separation: Effects on Mother-Infant Interaction One Year Later'. *Birth* (Berkeley, California), 36, pp. 97–109.

Christensson, Kyllike, T. Cabrera, E. Christensson, K. Uvnäs–Moberg and J. Winberg. (1995). 'Separation Distress Call in the Human Neonate in the Absence of Maternal Body Contact'. *Acta Paediatrica*, 84 (5), pp. 468–473.

Crenshaw, Jeannette T. (2014). 'Healthy Birth Practice# 6: Keep Mother and Baby Together—It's Best for Mother, Baby, and Breastfeeding'. *The Journal of Perinatal Education*, 23 (4), pp. 211–217.

Csaszar-Nagy, Noemi and Istvan Bokkon. (2018). 'Mother-Newborn Separation at Birth in Hospitals: A Possible Risk for Neurodevelopmental Disorders?' *Neuroscience and Biobehavioral Reviews*, 84, pp. 337–351.

Lynch, Catherine. (2021). 'Putting Children First: What Adoption Can Teach Us about Surrogacy'. In Marie-Josèphe Devillers and Ana-Luana Stoicea-Deram (Eds). *Towards the Abolition of Surrogate Motherhood*. Mission Beach: Spinifex Press.

Phillips, Raylene. (2013). 'The Sacred Hour: Uninterrupted Skin-to-Skin Contact Immediately After Birth'. *Newborn and Infant Nursing Reviews*, 13 (2), pp. 67–72.

Safari, Kolsoom, Awaz A. Saeed, Shukir S. Hasan and Lida Moghaddam-Benaem. (2018). 'The Effect of Mother and Newborn Early Skin-to-Skin Contact on Initiation of Breastfeeding, Newborn Temperature and Duration of Third Stage of Labor'. *International Breastfeeding Journal*, 13 (32). <https://internationalbreastfeedingjournal.biomedcentral.com/articles/10.1186/s13006-018-0174-9>.

Zakšek, Teja Š., Anita J. Došler, Ana P. Mivšek and Petra Petročnik. (2018). 'Neonatal Care in the First Hour of Life'. In R. Mauricio Barría (Ed.). *Selected Topics in Neonatal Care*, pp. 9–25.

International concern about baby misidentification in hospitals

de Souza Gomes, Adriana P., Danielle L. Querido, Gloria R. da Silva, Luana F. de Almeida and Ronilson G. Rocha. (2017). 'The Importance of Newborn Identification to the Delivery of Safe Patient Care'. *Cogitare Enferm*, 22 (3), e49501.

Ginsberg, Marc D. (2010). 'How Much Anguish is Enough—Baby Switching and Negligent Infliction of Emotional Distress'. *DePaul Journal of Health Care Law*, 13 (2), pp. 255–272.

Nelson, Tina E. (1999). 'Safeguarding Newborns: Managing the Risk'. *RN*, 62 (3), pp. 67–70.

Rizk, Khalil, Mariam Kayle and Lina Mekawi. (2009). 'Prevention of Infant Abductions and Mix-Ups in Hospitals'. *Human and Health*, 9, pp. 24–28.

Rusting, R. R. (2000). 'Baby Switching: An Underreported Problem that Needs to be Recognized'. *Journal of Healthcare Protection Management: Publication of the International Association for Hospital Security*, 17 (1), pp. 89–100.

Wallace, Susan C. (2016). 'Newborns Pose Unique Identification Challenges'. *Pennsylvania Patient Safety Advisory*, 13 (2), pp. 42–49.

Research on preventing baby misidentification

Balameenakshi, S. and S. Sumathi. (2013). 'Biometric Recognition of Newborns: Identification Using Footprints'. *2013 IEEE Conference on Information & Communication Technologies*.

Barra, Silvio, Andrea Casanova, Maria De Marsico and Daniel Riccio. (2014). 'Babies: Biometric Authentication of Newborn Identities by Means of Ear

Signatures'. *2014 IEEE Workshop on Biometric Measurements and Systems for Security and Medical Applications (BIOMS) Proceedings.*

Bharadwaj, Samarth, Himanshu S. Bhatt, Richa Singh, Mayank Vatsa and Sanjay K. Singh. (2010). 'Face Recognition for Newborns: A Preliminary Study'. *2010 Fourth IEEE International Conference on Biometrics: Theory, Applications and Systems (BTAS).*

Kushwaha, Riti, Neeta Nain and Gaurav Singal. (2017). 'Detailed Analysis of Footprint Geometry for Person Identification'. *2017 13th International Conference on Signal-Image Technology and Internet-Based Systems (SITIS).*

Other books by Spinifex Press

Adoption Deception: A Personal and Professional Journey
Penny Mackieson

What is it like to be adopted, have your identity changed and never feel quite at home in your new family, despite being loved? What is it like to become a social worker and be faced with the challenges and consequences of other adoptions every day? What is it like to hear the moving National Apology for Forced Adoptions by Prime Minister Julia Gillard in 2013 only to be faced a few months later by a new prime minister intent on forgetting all the lessons learnt and championing a deregulated parent-centred market-driven adoption industry?

Penny Mackieson takes us on her journey with the unique perspective of both an adopted person and a professional who worked in intercountry adoption for over a decade. She unravels the complexities, debunks the myths, analyses the policies and raises important questions about the ethical and human rights dilemmas in adoption.

Adoption Deception: A Personal and Professional Journey is a passionate, heart-wrenching and unflinchingly honest account of one woman's life as an adopted person and her campaign for change. The author presents a compelling argument for Permanent Care instead of adoption for vulnerable children unable to be raised by their families in the light of continuing issues of exploitation, identity loss and the priority given to adults' wishes over children's rights.

Adoption Deception *is a deeply personal account of the experience of adoption, and the effect it can have into adulthood. It is a story of how family relationships can be influenced by adoption policies and practices. It challenges us to think about how we respond to the 'commercialisation of children' through adoption and assisted reproductive technologies.*
—Professor Marie Connolly, Chair and Head of Social Work,
  The University of Melbourne

ISBN 9781742199740

*If you would like to know more about
Spinifex Press, write to us for a free catalogue, visit our
website or email us for further information
on how to subscribe to our monthly newsletter.*

Spinifex Press
PO Box 105
Mission Beach QLD 4852
Australia
www.spinifexpress.com.au
women@spinifexpress.com.au